Post-College
SURVIVAL

The essential money skills
you need to make it
on your own.

Macmillan Spectrum/Alpha Books
A Division of Macmillan General Reference
A Simon & Schuster Macmillan Company
1633 Broadway
New York, NY 10019

Library of Congress Cataloging-in-Publication Data: 96-078160

ISBN: 0-02-861549-2

99 98 97   8 7 6 5 4 3 2 1

Interpretation of the printing code: the rightmost number of the first series of numbers is the year of the book's printing; the rightmost number of the second series of numbers is the number of the book's printing. For example, a printing code of 97-1 shows that the first printing occurred in 1997.

Printed in the United States of America

Publisher: Theresa Murtha
Editor in Chief: Richard J. Staron
Production Editors: Lynn Northrup and John Carroll
Copy Editor: Linda Seifert
Cover Designer: Rachael McBrearty
Designer: Scott Meola
Production Team: Tammy Ahrens, Jerry Cole, Michelle Croninger, Toi Davis,
         Deb Kincaid, Kevin MacDonald, Angel Perez, Linda Qugley

TABLE OF CONTENTS

ACKNOWLEDGMENTS

I am very grateful to Alice Barrett and Rhonda Shapiro-Rieser for their encouragement, to the staff of Macmillan Spectrum for their assistance, and to the many individuals and organizations who provided me with the interviews and data necessary to make this handbook relevant.

Jo-Ann Johnston

Chapter 1

Getting Smart About Money

Some people say in a nonchalant way that they just aren't good with money. Some people say they're not good with money in a tone that's desperate, almost like a question. Of the two groups, a member of the second group is the kind of person who is better off. At least they realize they need to know something about money. The first group may want to go through life oblivious to financial concerns, preferring not to deal with them, but the truth is, they have no choice.

The consumer's range of choices in learning about money is like the motorist's array of choices in knowing about cars. If you get a license and start driving, you'll find out there are certain things you'll have to manage to keep the car operating, such as changing the oil, choosing the right tires, and having all the current automobile registration and inspection stickers legally required by your state. Managing your finances is like that in many ways. You've now started your working life, and you can think of your earnings and money-managing capacities as the financial engine that gets you to where you want to go in life. All along the way, you have to tend to the engine. You don't

1

GUIDELINES FOR MAKING FINANCIAL DECISIONS

1. Clarify the decision as much as possible, for example:

   ⇨ Do I take this job even though it pays less than I want?

   ⇨ Do I buy this car?

   ⇨ Do I invest this inheritance money in this particular investment?

   ⇨ Do I sell my stereo?

2. Realistically determine how much time you have to make the choice.

3. Determine whether you have enough information to make the decision. If not, work within your time frame to find the most reliable sources of information pertinent to the decision as you have framed it.

4. Clarify again, if necessary, exactly what decision you face.

5. Weigh the pros and cons of your alternatives, now and in three months, in six months, and if possible or relevant, in a year to three years. Think about a fallback plan if it turns out you don't like the decision, for example:

   ⇨ Can I get a salary review in six months if I agree to a lower salary figure now?

   ⇨ Can I get repairs under warranty on this car if I'm not sure about its reliability?

   ⇨ Can I shift the investment to something else later?

6. Look at your decision again—whatever it is—in a few months to see if there is any new information available to you now or any new insights that would mean going to the fallback plan, or that would at least help in the future if you have to make a similar choice again.

have to become a mechanical genius to keep a car moving well, unless you want to. Similarly, you won't need to become a fiscal wizard to manage your money suitably for your life. But you can't ignore the impact personal finance issues will have on your life either. There are some fundamentals that everyone needs to know to manage their money, such as understanding how much of your paycheck you're actually bringing home, knowing how to spend money wisely, handling borrowing effectively, and more. Just as importantly, working adults need the skills and the confidence that will help them understand changes that will occur at work or at home and affect their take-home pay. Or changes that might occur at their bank that could make it easier or harder for them to manage their accounts there. The world of personal finance is full of changes, major and minor, so you have to know how to evaluate the situation and make the best financial decisions for yourself. The checklist shown on the previous page can act as a guide to decision-making.

You may not have learned these things in college. You may not have learned this in your family, or from your friends either. If you did, count yourself as lucky. This book will add to what you already know. If you didn't get much guidance, don't worry; this book will cover the basics and help you get on the right track. If you're ready to start and become a money-smart person, congratulations. If you're uneasy with finances, let's discuss some of the sticking points where people sometimes allow themselves to stumble.

I'm Just Not Good with Money

In reality, you may not be too experienced with money. Or you may have made some mistakes with money in the past, like spending too much on stereo equipment in college and leaving yourself short on funds for textbooks. Or you might be afraid of making some dramatic missteps now that you're earning more money, and consequently have bigger sums to take care of—or to lose track of.

But even if all of this is true, even if you've been embarrassed or criticized over your money management in the past, that doesn't mean your course in life is set. Mistakes are how you learn, and past errors will not doom you forever. Even professionals in the world of finance have to learn through trial and error, like seeing if investing in a particular country's economy is a good idea. If you look at it that way, you'll find that buying a piece of furniture on impulse, and regretting the expense or finance charges later, is not the worst thing that you can do. This is not to make light of the kinds of financial holes people can dig themselves into. But you can recover from mistakes, especially if your attitude is that you're willing to think about your experiments with money after the fact, and see if you can identify any new information you learned that will help you in the future. This means learning from your experiences in a constructive way and adapting, instead of blaming yourself so unforgivingly for a bad judgment call that you're paralyzed with fear of financial management in the future.

You have the opportunity and the tools to improve your money management skills, no matter what level you're at now.

I'm Not Good at Math

This may be true, but it's beside the point. (Any fears you have about math aptitude are likely to be overblown, anyway.) Math and money aren't quite as intertwined as you may think. Beside the point? Yes. Lots of the fundamental questions about money management start with "What . . . " or "Is it . . . ," not "Find the square root of . . . " We're talking values and choices and priorities, and to some extent, strategies. Calculations are subordinate. So if you were to visit a financial planner or some other type of adviser, he'd probably ask you a lot about goals. In the early stages of a working life, those kinds of questions boil down to things like these:

- What kind of housing do you have now and what kind of housing do you want to live in in the future? A house with roommates, a rented apartment, a condo, or house you'd like to own?

- What kind of training or other degrees do you have to pursue in your field to keep your earning power up?

- Is it more important to you to have free time or extra money from a job with over-time or long hours?

These are the kinds of things you need to ask yourself first and think about.

Notice we haven't delved into any advanced math yet. It doesn't matter whether you passed solid geometry in high school, or if you limped through algebra in college, when you're contemplating whether it's more important for your mental health to take a vacation in Florida or to earn extra money working at another job when you have time off.

Yes, you do have calculations to make, but these days it's much easier to make them with checkbooks that come with calculators, or personal finance computer programs like Quicken or Microsoft Money that handle mathematics for you. In many instances, the computations are simple and you're adding, subtracting, multiplying, and dividing. Sometimes there is interest to figure, but you can get help doing that too (we'll touch on this more in Chapter 6). In fact, you may find you feel more confident and practiced in your math aptitude to the extent that managing your finances gives you an oppor-tunity to practice math concepts.

TIDBIT: One-third of a group of 800 people between the ages of 25 and 34, surveyed in June 1996 for the American Stock Exchange, said they use money management software.

So mathematics proficiency, or lack of it, isn't really a stumbling block or an overrid-ing concern. It's another factor in the equation, so to speak, but one that you can find a way to handle.

I Don't Have Enough Money to Bother with All This

To go back to our car analogy, that's sort of like saying I won't worry about changing my oil because I drive a Geo Metro instead of a Lexus. Everyone needs a grasp of the fundamentals, just as every vehicle, whether it's a budget car or a luxury auto, needs an oil change.

It's true that if you have a simpler financial profile—a job and only basic expenses to cover—you'll have fewer options to handle your money and therefore less to be confused by. On the other side of the coin though, you've got less room for mistakes. If housing costs eat up one-third to a half of your monthly income, you've got less flexibility in your budget for other things. To put it another way, if you've got $140 left after you sign the rent check, you've got to be a lot more careful and savvy than the person with $1,000 in his account after the rent check.

Besides, you don't want to get trapped in dead-end thinking. If you're only pulling in a small amount of pay now, but want to be earning more later, it makes sense to grow your money management thinking along with your career and income-producing plans. If you think you'll move into a better paying job in a couple of years, or that you might get a raise in six months, it's a good idea to have in mind where you'd like to apply that money, whether it's toward better housing or extra payments on student loans. You want your skills and readiness to keep pace with life's events, not to lag behind them.

Money Is the Root of All Evil

"Money is the root of all evil" is actually a misquote of a saying from the Bible that has taken on a life of its own. The original saying was that love of money is the root of all evil—not use of money, not earning of money, and not saving or investing money. There is quite a difference there.

Proper quotations aside, lots of people have a problem with money, whether they derive their concerns from religious text or from some other source. They feel that contact with money or thinking about money renders a person greedy and evil. So maybe they don't pay attention to where their money goes and they're broke all the time, but that doesn't give them a moral high ground. If you dislike materialism, and ride a bike to work, refuse to pollute, use as little cash as possible and send the rest of your earnings to charity, that's different. Then you're deciding what part you'll play in the economy and how you'll play it, instead of simply foundering in ignorance with pretensions of purity.

The bottom line is, money is neither good nor bad. How people use money and the attitudes people hold toward it are the keys. Money doesn't call the shots. Money itself doesn't make someone greedy. Money is simply the medium of exchange we use in the modern world because we don't find it convenient to trade furs anymore. It's more practical for us to use cash or substitutes for cash that can flow in and out of different bank accounts, different states, even different countries, if need be. If you're afraid of being tempted by large sums of money, that's not money's fault, and thinking that it is won't solve your problem with temptation. Further, possessing good money management skills won't make you obsess about money all the time. If you do obsess, there's another problem, but neglecting your financial affairs won't solve it—it eventually will just create another mess.

The problems of corruption, greed, and neuroses are for others to explore. But if you're looking for a pragmatic, workable attitude to adopt towards money, consider this one: Money is just a tool. How you use it is up to you. It is clear that having use of this tool gives you more flexibility: Having more money gives you more options on how to live your life; having less of it shortens that list of options.

Somebody Else Is Going to Take Care of This for Me

That may have been true while you were growing up, and your family or guardians handled the most fundamental responsibilities like shelter and food, but in general, adulthood means keeping track of your own finances.

Some people do have relationships where one person handles the finances, be it a partner or spouse. Your partner or spouse has an aptitude for money, you can't stand balancing a checkbook—the excuses go on. This isn't a wise policy. Some household chores can be split up and delegated, but the reality is that everyone needs basic financial survival skills. Look at your parent's or grandparent's generations, and see what happens when people divorce, become ill, or, in the very worst scenario, die. The people left behind will tell you that if they didn't know how to handle money before a problem arose, they found themselves ill-prepared to learn a whole new set of skills when they were coping with a life shift that in itself was bewildering and draining. That's the safety reason for having both people in a couple be financially aware.

But even when there's no catastrophe looming, some people will tell you it sure makes day-to-day life easier when both people in a couple know how to handle finances, including both the monthly bill-paying and thinking about the long-term future. Maybe the person who balances the checkbook or pays the utilities every month would like a break from that chore occasionally, while being secure in the knowledge that the checkbook balance will be recorded accurately and the bills will be mailed on time. It can be a relief to rotate these chores occasionally, and doing so also can give each partner a better appreciation of what it takes to sustain the household.

Also, it seems to help to have a peer with whom you can discuss long- and short-term financial matters. It helps to learn together, and to understand more fully what each of you wants from life. (Even if you're single, or not in a relationship, it's a relief to have a friend you can discuss money matters with, so you can compare experiences and ideas.)

Some clever souls may be thinking, ah, I'll hire someone to take care of all this for me. You think you'll get an accountant to do your taxes, but what about the month-to-month bill paying and recording of income and deductions? The accountant has to know what to figure, after all. You can speed up bookkeeping with a computer program, but you still have to enter the data and make the choices. You can hire someone as a personal financial manager, turn over all your bills and access to your checking accounts, but does that really make you feel secure? Every so often a high-profile actor or musician who has done that turns around and sues the manager. It makes the news, and the celebrity says that while he or she was concentrating on artistic pursuits, the manager was entrusted with the finances, but in fact stole or mismanaged the money, the artist later discovered. That's the risk of abdicating responsibility.

Or take investments. You say you'll get an adviser, but you still need to decide for yourself, and communicate to your adviser, how much financial risk you can stand and what kinds of goals you want to attain.

Simply put, there's no way to avoid financial matters for very long, and when you forego that responsibility, you run the risk of mishap.

Summary

If you wanted to, you could probably still come up with more reasons—rationalizations, really—to avoid understanding money. But why? Clearly, it's a survival skill everyone needs. Further, you may find it enjoyable to learn about a new area, or at least boost your confidence level to realize that you've added a valuable skill to your knowledge base.

Action Items

Start looking in the media—newspapers, TV, radio, cable stations, and magazines—for financial reporting you can understand and enjoy, and follow it regularly.

Cultivate a buddy with whom you can comfortably broach financial topics. You won't be "prying" into matters of pay, you'll be comparing deals on the best banks, strategies, and so on.

Invest in a calculator-type of checkbook register, a computer program, or even both. These tools can help you with the nitty-gritty details of tracking money.

Keep in mind that money is a tool, a powerful tool, but that you're in charge of the job of shaping your life, your spending, and your earnings.

CASE IN POINT:

Building Your Confidence

In October 1996, *The Boston Globe* printed a profile of a young man who seemed poised to make a good living in the business world, even though he came from a working-class family and had to learn about money and finance.

His name is Felix Soto Jr. and at 25 he is a student at Northeastern University and owner of J & M Auto Sales, which sells used foreign cars in the Jamaica Plain section of Boston.

Soto told interviewer Alisa Valdes that when he was younger, he "used to watch my parents get up at six in the morning to take the train to minimum-wage jobs, and they'd always come home depressed and defeated, with hardly any money . . . they worked harder than anyone I knew, and never had much to show for it. I never wanted a life like that."

Soto found a mentor to help him in the used car business. This mentor showed him how to get a license to sell cars, how to get the financing from banks to buy used cars to resell, and also how to build his business and hire employees. Soto told *The Globe* reporter, at first he felt intimidated. "I was like 'Oh no.' I was scared. I had never dealt with a bank. I had no credit. I thought that was like the white man's world. I had this idea that they would be doing me a favor. (His mentor) taught me that they weren't. Now I know that they needed me as much as I needed them."

Chapter 2

Paychecks, Job Benefits, and Taxes

Most people aren't going to win the lottery or a magazine sweepstakes, but instead will have to build financial security from week to week, month to month.

A good place to start is in reviewing your employee benefits and paycheck stub to make sure you understand everything that goes into your compensation. Sometimes people make the mistake of looking only at the cash they receive for working, but benefits experts say that programs like employer-sponsored health insurance, vacation pay, and other benefits can be worth a third or more of the overall compensation you may get as a full-time employee. That's why it's important to know what comes in your employee package, to be sure you're making the best use of all your different forms of compensation. In some work settings, the employee benefits manuals are still hard to fathom, and it may take some work to plow through them to understand what you're getting, or it may take some discussion with your supervisor. You also need to pay close attention to your paystub for information about your pay and deductions from your pay.

This has been easier in the past few years as many companies have worked to make their paystubs better labeled and more clearly understandable.

```
HARMON PERSONNEL SERVICES, INC. 04-96 to 02-10-96      YEAR-TO-DATE** SS# 014-54-205395
JOH926  Jo-Ann Johnston                              Regular Pay Rate 0.000
Reg-Hrs  37.500  Reg-Pay        281.25  Reg-Hrs  37.500  Reg-Pay        281.25
OT-Hrs    0.000  OT-Pay           0.00  OT-Hrs    0.000  OT-Pay           0.00
DT-Hrs    0.000  DT-Pay           0.00  DT-Hrs    0.000  DT-Pay           0.00
Tot-Hrs  37.500  Tot-Pay        281.25  Tot-Hrs  37.500  Tot-Pay        281.25
    Federal Withheld            -27.26      Federal Withheld            -27.26
    State Withheld              -13.17      State Withheld              -13.17
    Social Sec. Withheld        -17.44      Social Sec. Withheld        -17.44
    Medicare Withheld            -4.08      Medicare Withheld            -4.08




    Cust: GOL150 37.5 Reg at 7.50

            Net Pay          $219.30                  Net Pay          $219.30
```

Courtesy of Paychex Inc.

Starting Pay in Recent Years	
Accountant	$27,900 (bachelor's degree) and $31,500 (master's degree)
Engineer	$34,100 (bachelor's degree) and $40,200 (master's degree)
Librarian	$28,300 (master's degree)
Geologist	$27,900
Paralegal	$14,000 to $32,000
Travel agent	$12,990

Source: Occupational Outlook Handbook, 1996–97 Edition. *Compiled by the United States Department of Labor.*

The easiest way to talk about some of the most common deductions is by looking at a hypothetical example, and then illustrating other possible deductions or benefits. The American Payroll Association, a nonprofit educational group, explained this fictional paystub for someone who lives in Boston, is single, has no dependents, and gets paid every other week. The worker has a gross annual salary of $35,000, meaning before anything gets taken out, that's how much pay is allotted. This person works on salary—that's different from hourly pay. Salaried workers are expected to work as many hours a

Form **W-4**	**Employee's Withholding Allowance Certificate**	OMB No. 1545-0010
Department of the Treasury Internal Revenue Service	▶ **For Privacy Act and Paperwork Reduction Act Notice, see reverse.**	**1995**

1 Type or print your first name and middle initial	Last name	2 Your social security number

Home address (number and street or rural route)	3 ☐ Single ☐ Married ☐ Married, but withhold at higher Single rate. **Note:** *If married, but legally separated, or spouse is a nonresident alien, check the Single box.*
City or town, state, and ZIP code	4 If your last name differs from that on your social security card, check here and call 1-800-772-1213 for a new card . . . . . ▶ ☐

5	Total number of allowances you are claiming (from line G above or from the worksheets on page 2 if they apply) .	**5**	
6	Additional amount, if any, you want withheld from each paycheck	**6**	$
7	I claim exemption from withholding for 1995 and I certify that I meet **BOTH** of the following conditions for exemption:		

- Last year I had a right to a refund of **ALL** Federal income tax withheld because I had **NO** tax liability; **AND**
- This year I expect a refund of **ALL** Federal income tax withheld because I expect to have **NO** tax liability.

If you meet both conditions, enter "EXEMPT" here . . . . ▶ | **7** |

Under penalties of perjury, I certify that I am entitled to the number of withholding allowances claimed on this certificate or entitled to claim exempt status.

Employee's signature ▶

Date ▶ , 19

8 Employer's name and address (Employer: Complete 8 and 10 only if sending to the IRS)	9 Office code (optional)	10 Employer identification number

Cat. No. 10220Q

week as the employer needs. (More on that later.) So, this person went to work, and first filed a W-4 form, provided by someone in payroll, the supervisor, or maybe someone in human resources.

W-4, the Employee's Withholding Allowance Certificate, is a federal form. This form tells your employer how much money you want held back from your check each pay period and turned over to different government taxing authorities. This helps you pay your income taxes on a plan, and, gets the money to the government quickly. In fact, 70 percent of the money the federal government collects comes from paychecks, according to the American Payroll Association. Lots of people still pay taxes when they file their annual income tax return on or before April 15, but the goal is to have enough held back from your pay, so that you're roughly equal with the government come April. You don't owe them any more money, and they don't owe you any more money (paid in the form of a refund). Sure, some people like getting tax refunds because it's a check for a lump sum, but accountant after accountant will tell you that's not so great. If you're getting a refund, you've been letting the government use some of your money for months, and you haven't been getting any interest for providing this loan. Meanwhile, you could have been putting that money to use elsewhere, buying something you needed, paying a bill, investing it, or putting it in a savings account to gain interest. It's important to make sure you're getting things correct on your W-4— to make sure your taxes are being paid in the right amounts. Then, when you file your annual income tax return, you won't have any surprises.

So, this worker is single, and has no one else depending on him or her for support. Knowing that, along with knowing the pay, the employer can figure out how much to hold back for taxes. The worker claims only one withholding allowance, or exemption, because he is single and has no dependents. This is a bit technical, but makes sense. All workers are allowed to say that some of their pay should not be subject to federal tax—the law assumes that money is for self support. The more people you have depending on you, the more allowances you need to take. If you have a spouse who isn't working and you have two children, you need to take four allowances, one for each person in the household. If you are married, but your spouse is working, your partner takes his or her own allowance on his or her own W-4. Working parents have to decide who claims the children for tax purposes. If you're working more than one job, you may need help figuring out how much pay to have held back for taxes so that you don't owe a balance at the end of the year. If your family changes, or you find there's been a mistake on how you filled out your W-4, you can fill out a new one. In some cases, you have to fill out the new form within 10 days of a change.

TIDBIT: If this is still confusing to you, ask your employer for IRS Publication 919, "Is My Withholding Correct?" or call the IRS toll-free at 1-800-829-3676. You'll get a copy of the publication and can use the instructions to review the specifics of your situation.

Worker: Single, No Dependents, Making $35,000 a Year, Paid Biweekly	
Gross pay	$1,346.15
401(k) retirement savings plan	$53.85
Federal income tax	$223.09
Social Security tax	$83.46
Medicare tax	$19.52
State (Mass.) income tax	$70.76
Net pay	$895.47

Gross pay. We arrived at this figure by taking the annual salary of $35,000 and dividing it by 26, for the number of pay periods in a year for a worker paid every other week.

401(k) retirement savings plan. This is one of the most common, and growing, ways to save for retirement. It used to be more common for companies to take responsibility for putting aside money for a worker's pension, and then investing that money. Now, more of that responsibility is shifting to workers through 401(k) plans at companies in the private sector, and their counterparts, 403(b) plans in jobs in education and government. Participating in a 401(k) plan is voluntary, but we're assuming this worker has it on the ball: He or she knows this is a great way to build up some retirement savings, and that the earlier you start, the better, because you have more years to let your money build.

It works like this: You tell your company how much of your pay, on a percentage basis, you want put into the plan. The money gets taken out of your gross pay—up to certain limits set by law—and you don't pay any taxes on those earnings until you retire and withdraw the money you saved. This worker is saving four percent of his or her gross pay, which is in the typical range of four to six percent, according to R. Theodore Benna, president of the 401(k) Association. That comes to $53.85 every pay period for this worker. Benna says it's better for workers in their 20s and 30s to save 10 percent of their pay.

According to Benna, some employers will match some of the pay you set aside in your retirement account, most often with a match between 25 cents to 50 cents on every employee dollar saved. Even if you don't save 10 percent, at the very least it's smart, Benna says, to save enough to get any matching money the employer offers. Otherwise, he notes, you're just throwing away the matching funds available to you.

Federal income tax. There are a number of different methods to figure federal tax from which employers can choose. Basically, your federal income tax is based on how much gross pay you make, how often you get paid, and whether you're married, and takes into account subtractions or pre-tax deductions like 401(k) plans and your withholding allowances.

Social Security tax. Employees have a percentage of their gross salary (6.2 percent of salary up to $62,700 in 1996) held from gross pay to pay current and future benefits to current retirees, disabled adults, surviving spouses, and minor dependents of deceased workers. If your retired grandmother gets a monthly Social Security check, it's from this system. Employers match the sum that employees have deducted, although that matching number doesn't show up on the check.

Many politicians are concerned that the Social Security system is going broke, that it won't be able to take in enough money to pay for future retirees—people like you when you're retired. It's impossible to predict exactly how the system may be retooled, but it is an important political and personal finance issue. Maybe you won't be able to do much about how the system changes or how well it works, but keep in mind one thing: Social Security was never meant to be the only source of income in someone's retirement, although some people have used it that way. It would be folly to plan that way today, especially if the system is financially stressed. That's why it's important to begin saving early through other means for retirement, like the 401(k) plans.

The Social Security Administration advises if you switch jobs often, check to make sure your payroll deductions for Social Security have been correctly recorded to the government and attributed to you. An error, perhaps in recording your Social Security number at a given job, can confuse your records. And it's easier to straighten out mistakes now, instead of 30 years from now, when an employer might have gone out of business and no one is around to verify that you worked there for three years. Check this by requesting a free document called the Personal Earnings and Benefits Estimate

Statement from the Social Security Administration. It's a form you fill out, return to SSA, and then they return the information they have on file for you. It's also a valuable planning tool that older people in your family might want to request so they can see what they can expect to get in Social Security on retirement.

Medicare tax. This government insurance program pays for health care for people older than 65, people who have been collecting Social Security disability for at least two years, and people who have suffered kidney failure.

A percentage of your gross salary is held to pay for Medicare benefits: 1.45 percent of salary in 1996, with no wage limit. Social Security and Medicare together comprise 7.65 percent of your gross pay. With employer matching amounts, about 15 percent of your gross pay is set aside for these funds. People who are self-employed have to come up with the whole 15 percent themselves from earnings. In the past, amounts taken out for these two items were sometimes lumped together and called FICA, for the Federal Insurance Contributions Act. (That's why sometimes you see joke buttons that say things like: "Who the hell is FICA and why does he take so much of my paycheck?" Now you know.) But now, these amounts are broken out into separate lines. The IRS collects this money and then distributes it to the correct agencies, along with the federal income tax.

State income tax. The state tax in Massachusetts is 5.95 percent of gross pay after the deductions for the 401(k), Social Security, and Medicare. In Massachusetts, the state tax goes into the Massachusetts General Fund to pay for state services, like roads. Many other states do the same, although there are some states, including New Hampshire, that have no state income tax. (That may look good on the surface, but it's also common for property owners in such states to pay higher local real estate taxes so communities can provide some of the services that state governments might otherwise provide.) In other cases, some states will show added separate taxes for specific items. Alaska, New Jersey, and Pennsylvania tax for state unemployment insurance to help workers who have lost their jobs. And California, Hawaii, New Jersey, New York, and Rhode Island tax for a fund to help workers who got hurt away from the job and temporarily are unable to earn money.

There's another possibility this example doesn't show: local income taxes that may be levied in some cities (like New York City) or in some counties, or on people who either live or work in the locale, depending on local laws.

Net pay. Okay, here's what's available for this worker to live on for two weeks, about two-thirds of the actual gross pay. This is how much you'd get at a bank for presenting this paycheck. Surprised? Lots of people are. In fact, in 1995, most people had to work until April 1 just to make enough money to cover their federal, state, and local income tax obligations, according to a Washington, D.C. group called the Tax Foundation.

Other Items That Might Have Shown Up on Your Paystub

Overtime pay. Some workers have to be paid extra, at the rate of one and one-half times their normal pay, for all hours worked over and above those in a work week (often 40 hours). Usually, people who work on an hourly basis are entitled to overtime pay. Salaried employees, like the worker in the example here, many white-collar administrators, professionals, and government employees aren't eligible for overtime. It's important to find out from your employer what your status is.

Overtime pay has become an important component of some people's personal lives and of the wider economy. Indeed, some households count on steady overtime to bring in enough money to meet expenses. Some employers would rather pay existing employees overtime on a long-running basis than hire new employees to take up the slack. That's because new employees may carry new benefit costs with them for the employer, and it may actually be cheaper to pay existing employees extra, even at the rate of time-and-a-half.

An alternative to overtime is compensatory time off—called comp time, which the employee could take when work conditions aren't so hectic, but usually in a given time schedule. It isn't a paystub category, but it is an important workplace issue. Politicians are debating on new and different rules that govern how and when companies can offer comp time to employees. Meanwhile, it's also important to get to know and understand the customs and expectations at your place of work.

Shift or differential pay. In some jobs, especially on late-night or early-morning shifts, you earn extra pay to compensate for the irregular hours.

Sick pay or vacation pay. Your paystub will generally note if you're being paid for time under your company's sick leave or vacation policy. Some paystubs now even show how much time you've taken under these categories so far, and how much you have left to use.

Workplaces have lots of variations in these policies, covering both how many days are available to you (they may increase after you've worked there for some time) and how you can use them. For example, say you have had an incredibly busy work year, and didn't take any sick time or time off for vacation. Some companies might let you "bank" those days and roll them over to the next year. Some may let you roll the vacation days over, but say, here's some cash for the sick days you didn't take. Some might say sorry folks, if you don't use them, you lose them. Know the policies where you work.

Medical or insurance benefits deductions. Your company might want you to pay for some of the costs (premiums) for your health insurance coverage, if you're lucky enough to get it as a benefit. This is a tough area for many young people, because sometimes they have to start in one or two part-time jobs and there may not be health insurance benefits. If you're self-employed you can buy your own, but you can only deduct part of the cost, and the percentage is increasing each year. In that case, you need to do what you can to get insurance: Look for another job, ask if you can get attached to a family member's policy, or investigate less expensive or short-term plans through local chambers of commerce (which can get you discounts if you join) or directly from insurance companies.

Sometimes employers offer life or disability insurance too, and may ask you to pay some of the cost. If you have any choice in benefits—maybe you have what is called a cafeteria plan and can pick what you need from an array of options, as compared to just getting a standardized package—this is one area to look at closely. Single people with no children don't generally need life insurance because there's no one depending on their income, and therefore no one who would need to replace it. But single people can get injured, in car accidents, for example, and be out of work for awhile, unable to earn pay. Disability insurance covers part of the income that's lost and is a good choice for protecting yourself against the financial pressures that a mishap would cause. If your employer doesn't offer disability insurance as a benefit, consider buying it on your own as soon as you're financially on your feet with a steady job and a measure of financial independence.

TIDBIT: What makes up a good benefits package? Starbucks Coffee Co., the chain of coffee shops that's based in Seattle, gets good press for paying for much of the medical coverage, hospitalization, vision, and dental care of employees, even part-time workers. Of course, they're not the only ones. National magazines often write about and rank companies with good benefits packages, good employee relations, and friendly working environments for various populations, such as working parents, people of color, and gays and lesbians. Low turnover at a company, compared to others in its industry, also is a good sign.

Fast-Growing Job Fields for College Graduates		
ASSOCIATE DEGREE	**BACHELOR'S DEGREE**	**MASTER'S DEGREE**
Paralegals	Systems analysts	Operations research analysts
Medical records technicians	Computer engineers	Speech-language pathologists and audiologists
Dental hygenists	Occupational therapists	Management analysts
Respiratory therapists	Physical therapists	Counselors
Radiologic technologists and technicians	Special education teachers	Urban and regional planners
Registered nurses	Elementary school teachers	
	Secondary school teachers	
	Social workers	

Source: Occupational Outlook Handbook, 1996–97 Edition. *Compiled by the United States Department of Labor.*

Flexible spending plans. These plans let you save pre-tax dollars in accounts for specific purposes. For example, this plan covers medical costs you paid out-of-pocket because they weren't covered by insurance or a deductible you might have to meet before your health insurance kicked in. Or, if you're a parent, it might reimburse you for money spent on day care for your child while you were working. These are good deals to take advantage of too, because you don't have to earn as much money to cover these bills as you would if you were using regular, taxable money—Uncle Sam would want his share of that. Find out the rules in your workplace for how much you can set aside, and how and when you can get money out of the accounts.

INVESTMENTS/EXPENSES OF JOB HUNTING

- Resume and cover letter preparation
    - ⇨ Professional service
    - ⇨ Software
    - ⇨ Books
    - ⇨ Stationery
    - ⇨ Postage
- Phone calls and a professional-sounding phone message recording system
- Portfolio of work, if needed
- Employment agency fees
- Periodicals and online services with job listings
- Appropriate interview attire
- Travel, meals, and lodging to job interviews and job fairs
- Time off from other work to go to job interviews and job fairs

TIDBIT: You can't deduct these expenses on your income taxes if they're for finding your first job, but keep the records so that you'll know what to expect next time. Some of these types of expenses may be deductible for finding later jobs. Keep abreast of the tax rules.

Other Forms of Compensation

Pay structures differ from job to job. Sales people often get some of their earnings through commissions rather than salary, so that part of their overall pay is derived from a percentage of how much they sell. Health care professionals may get some pay for being on call, that is, being ready to come in and work if needed. In that case, even if the employee isn't summoned to work, he or she is still paid for making themselves available for a given period of time.

Some other benefits don't show up on your paystub, but are available at some workplaces and are good for your pocketbook: Tuition reimbursement that covers part of the costs of additional training is one example. Profit sharing is another popular benefit with employees. It rewards workers for generating money for the company beyond company expenses by giving employees an extra check besides their usual pay.

What if You're an Independent Contractor Instead of an Employee?

In these days of uncertain employment, many companies use some people on a steady basis, but as freelance suppliers of labor or services. These workers don't get regular benefits or full-time pay, but it beats not working at all. Often, income is reported to you at the end of a year or the beginning of the following year on a Form 1099-MISC (MISC for miscellaneous income), as opposed to Form W-2, the Wage and Tax Statement. If you're in this situation, one of your goals will be to get paid enough to buy your own health insurance and disability policy, and to fund the other benefits you'd like, such as vacation pay or sick days. In essence, you'd need to make enough money so that you can afford to take some days off for illness or rest and relaxation. As your own employer, one of the things you must do is pay both the employee and the employer portions of the Social Security tax owed. This is a financial drain for many self-employed business people, but it must be done.

It's Tax Time

So you've had your tax obligations, we hope, withheld throughout the year. Or, if you're self-employed, you've been putting some of your pay aside in a separate account to pay for taxes. By October of any year, it's a good idea to check on your situation. Look at your paystubs, and see how much you've had withheld. Go to the library, and compare your situation with tax guides on file there. If it looks like you're having enough withheld to come out even, great. If you're afraid you're not having enough withheld from pay, or from self-employment earnings, this is the time to correct that. Either have more withheld, or try to get a self-employment project with the specific goal of devoting the pay to your set-aside fund for taxes. If you continue to be self-employed for the long-term, you're going to want to pay estimated taxes quarterly, probably with the help of an accountant. This will help you mimic the withholding system that company employees have. By compensating, or at least partly correcting any tax imbalance during the autumn, you're avoiding any surprise drains on your money in the early part of the following year when the tax balance is actually due. This is a difficult season for many people financially because of post-holiday bills and, in many areas of the country, heating bills.

By January 31 of the following year, each employer you've worked for has to send you a multiple copy Form W-2 for the previous year. This form shows how much you made, and how much in taxes was withheld from your checks. These statements give you the data you need to fill out the federal, state, and any local income tax returns.

Usually, as you enter the workforce, your tax profile is pretty uncomplicated—though moving from one state to another will add a wrinkle—and you can get by with filing the simplest tax forms. And lots of help is available each year from the IRS, in the media, from books and software, or from accountants or tax-preparation firms.

Actually filling out the forms requires that you've got some uninterrupted time, all your materials together, and a good frame of mind for working your way through, line by line. The following elements are important to understand because they crop up every year, and knowing about them will make filling out the forms easier and your financial planning smoother.

Adjusted Gross Income. This takes all your income into account, not just wages and salary, but also any interest you earned on investments, any money you may have made by selling stocks (called capital gains), unemployment insurance checks, and so on. Then that sum is reduced by certain expenses, perhaps money you put into an Individual Retirement Account (IRA), or if you are self-employed, money paid for health insurance premiums. Moving expenses for relocating for another job, and not

COMMON MISTAKES ON TAX RETURNS

- Names or Social Security numbers that don't agree with IRS records

- Arithmetic mistakes, such as misplaced decimal points

- Numbers on the wrong line

- Missing W-2 forms

- The wrong filing status, determined by your marital status and family situation

- The wrong standard deduction, which depends on your marital status and other factors

- Returns sent without a signature, a return address, or enough postage

Source: IRS

reimbursed to you by an employer, also are included in this category. Tax professionals call these "above-the-line deductions"—calculated before the adjusted gross income, or AGI. Above-the-line deductions reduce tax liability more than other deductions. When all these sources of income and adjustments are taken into consideration, then you've got your adjusted gross income. To reduce your taxes, you have to find ways to reduce your AGI. That's why IRAs, for instance, are still popular among financial advisers, because they can reduce a person's tax liability in a given year within certain income earning limits, and also help them build a source of money for later in life.

Exemptions. The IRS lets you shield a certain amount of income for supporting yourself, and any other dependents, such as children. When you figure your federal income taxes, you deduct these exemptions from the AGI to get to the final amount of taxable income.

Deductions. Deductions also are subtracted from the AGI to get to the final taxable income, because the government reasons that everyone needs to have some money for certain expenses, like job- or business-related expenses and medical bills. Everybody gets tax deductions, it's just that some get more than others. Each year you decide what category of deduction works for you. If you've got a fairly straightforward financial situation, you'll probably take the *standard deduction*, an amount the government figures for you to cover daily living expenses such as medical attention, donations to charity, costs of things you need for your job, and so on. If you claim *itemized deductions*, more money will be sheltered from taxes than if you took the standard deduction. But they're harder to claim. The point behind itemizing is to give credit to people who spent more than the standard deduction compensates for. There are rules: You have to have spent more than the specific financial thresholds the government sets. For example, you may want to deduct your medical expenses, but the government says you can only deduct those that come to more than 7.5 percent of your AGI. If your medical bills were high, say, $1,000 in one year, and your AGI was $15,000, you still couldn't take a specific medical deduction. That's because 7.5 percent of the $15,000 (.075 × 15,000) comes to $1,125. If your medical bills had been $1,130, you could only deduct $5.00—the amount above the AGI. (This reality is what makes those flexible spending accounts attractive—they let you put away pre-tax money to pay for medical expenses your insurance won't cover.) Miscellaneous expenses, including union dues, work uniforms, subscriptions to periodicals in your work field, and more educational courses that improve your job skills, can also be deducted. But miscellaneous expenses have to come to more than 3 percent of the AGI. So in the example of someone with $15,000 in AGI, the miscellaneous expenses you can deduct are only the ones that come to more than $450 (.03 × 15,000). That might work during a year when you're taking an additional course at a community college—one that your employer isn't reimbursing you for— but otherwise, that's a lot of magazine subscriptions.

The effect of these thresholds on deductions is that lots of people can't meet them. They end up taking the standard deduction, even if it seems to them that they had lots of expenses. One strategy that sometimes works for some people is to take a take a standard deduction in some years, and to take itemized in other years when there are more expenses than normal.

Other Tax Lingo Worth Knowing

Whenever politicians talk about the tax system, they'll refer to terms that you should know about, especially if they talk about changing any of these elements of the system. For example, a *tax credit* will save the taxpayer more money than a *tax deduction*, because tax deductions get watered down by other required formulas. There are fewer tax credits allowed than tax deductions.

Tax brackets refer to percentage levels set to compute taxes, such as 15 percent, 28 percent, 31 percent, 36 percent, and 39.6 percent. The higher your income, the higher your tax bracket will be. In the United States, as of 1991, most workers were paying 25 percent of their income in income and payroll taxes, compared to 33 percent paid by workers in other industrialized countries, according to the Organization for Economic Cooperation and Development.

The marriage tax penalty is a quirk that means two people earning incomes who marry pay more in taxes than if they just lived together and filed individual returns.

Action Items

Start storing your paystubs in their own place.

....

Get a copy of your company's employee benefits manual, or listing, and read it over periodically to make sure you understand everything. Keep it updated with any clippings you collect from employee newsletters.

....

Make a friend somewhere in administration or human resources, someone who can provide reliable information when you've got a question. Always be polite and thank them for their help: Often people in these jobs are presented with plenty of problems and it's smart to show them that you appreciate their help.

....

Learn where the IRS and Social Security offices are in your area so you'll know where to go for help if you need it. Also check out the reference desks of public and college libraries for tax instructions and other information on these subjects.

....

Keep copies of all your tax returns for three to five years. You may not get audited, but they're handy to have for other things, like proving income for loans.

CASE IN POINT:

From Paystub to Tax Return

If we look at the case we created for the paystub figured by the American Payroll Association, we can see how payroll information feeds directly into the tax return. The example featured a single person in Boston earning $35,000 annually. The worker got paid every other week, having $223.09 taken out of every check for federal taxes, and having $53.85 sheltered in a 401(k) retirement savings plan, or $1,400 each year. That $1,400 does not show up on the worker's W-2, as the money is not considered taxable income in the year earned. We'll assume the worker didn't have any other income, even interest income from bank accounts or adjustments like moving expenses. Here are the important figures and entries for the worker, based on guidelines for income from 1995.

Filing status:	Single
Exemptions:	1
Wages:	$33,600
AGI:	$33,600
Standard deduction:	$3,900
Exemptions (1):	$2,500
Taxable income:	$27,200

Taxable income = AGI minus standard deduction, and minus exemption amount

Chapter 3

Handling Cash and Bank Accounts

Now that you're working full time,
you'll have more money flowing in and out of your checking account than before. So even though you are used to handling a checking account, and hopefully, keeping track of your balance, now is a good time to look at some additional strategies for handling your cash flow.

Finding a Checking Account

First, you'll need to decide where you're going to park the money you'll be using to pay your regular living expenses. That's right, park it. Your average checking account, or share account as they are called at credit unions, is really a place to move money in and out of for the short-term. (You select other kinds of financial products for long-term savings or investments. These will be detailed in Chapter 12.)

SUBSTITUTES FOR CASH AND PERSONAL CHECKS

Electronic Transfers—These transfers take money out of your checking account, usually for a regular amount at set intervals to move money or pay a business. You can use transfers to move money out of checking and into an investment or savings account, for example, or to make a monthly payment on a car loan, for auto insurance, for a health club fee, or to a computer online service.

Money Orders—Money orders work like checks. You can buy them from a bank or post office, or from many convenience or grocery stores, for the amount of the order, plus a small fee. Money orders will clear faster for the recipient than personal checks.

Cashier's Checks or Certified Checks—These checks, obtained at banks, are like money orders, but for larger amounts. They may be required for a down payment for a car, for example.

Traveler's Checks—Traveler's checks are handy on vacations and available at banks and credit unions for a fee. They come in preset denominations, such as $20, $50, and so on.

Debit Cards—Debit cards look like credit cards or ATM cards but take the money right out of a bank account.

Stored Value Cards—These cards are sold by denomination. You swipe them through a machine to deduct the value of a purchase. Stored value cards are handier than carrying around change for small daily purchases you might make at vending machines.

Bank Accounts Compared

DEPOSIT ACCOUNTS	CHECKING ACCOUNTS
Variety of savings accounts	Variety of checking accounts
Basic, no minimum deposit, no fees	Charge monthly fees
Minimum deposits, may be fees for falling below	Charge fees per check over a certain number, such as when you write more than 10 a month
Holiday savings or vacation clubs, regular deposits, simple terms	Charge fees if you don't keep a certain balance
	No fees or charges to certain customers, or from certain institutions

Certificates of Deposit (CDs)

CDs are offered for a fixed deposit amount, and with a fixed date for taking money out (the maturity date). In return, the customer earns a certain interest rate.

Money Market Deposit Accounts

This is usually a savings account that lets you write some checks if you need to, so it's kind of a hybrid. It's a place to park lots of money, say more than $1,000, for a short term to get the best interest rate possible, or to stash cash that you need to have quick access to, but don't know exactly when you'll need it, such as an emergency fund.

If you think of the checking account as a parking lot or garage, you'll get a better sense of some of the issues involved in selecting an institution and then managing the account.

For example, you want to park close to home and to work, correct? You'll want to do the same with your money, for convenience sake. And just as you may hunt for a parking space that's easy to enter and exit, you also may want to look for a bank in the areas you frequent with enough automated-teller machines, so that you can easily handle deposits, withdrawals, or other functions like moving money between accounts or checking your balance. Convenience is more of an issue with checking accounts than other bank accounts. Some people like having a savings account at an institution that's removed from their normal travels; that way they can deposit by mail but not be so tempted to withdraw money. And it doesn't really matter so much where you get a car loan, especially if you don't intend to make the payments in person, but by mail or electronic transfer instead.

Costs and services of banking are linked considerations. Often with banking services, prices are attached to a bundle of services that may or may not apply to you. For example, maybe you can get free checking—no monthly charges—if you keep a high balance in your account. But if it's unrealistic to think that you're going to have $1,000 lying dormant, and that even if you had it, it would be in a checking account, then that offer is no good to you. So typically you'll compare other considerations: Is there a charge every month or every time you write a check? Is there a charge for using ATM machines that other banks own or that your own bank owns? Some big banks even charge for talking to a human teller. In the past few years, banks have been trying to rake in more money through these fees, so it's important to compare and to watch the announcements that come to you from the bank—these may be announcing new fees that will be tacked onto your account.

In general, credit unions are less expensive to use than banks. They're member-owned cooperatives whose mission is to make enough money to keep the institution going, and reward their customer-members with any other profits. This contrasts with for-profit banks that need to make enough money to cover operations and generate money for the owners or shareowners. But first, you have to be able to join a credit union, either because you belong to a certain population like an employee group, a religious affiliation, or a locale, or because you are related to someone who is a member. You can't just walk in off the street as you can with a bank, because credit unions limit memberships to certain populations.

Using your Sharechek register

Your Sharechek register is your record of the checks you have written, the deposits, and the transfers you have made, and how much money is left in the account.

When you receive your initial order of Sharecheks, and each time you reorder, you will receive a Sharechek register which fits into the Sharechek cover with your Sharecheks and can be replaced, as needed.

When you begin each new register, be sure to fill in the information on the cover of the register. This will aid in record-keeping and at tax time.

Register Number _____ *13*

This register contains the records of items numbered

From _____ *1895* To _____ *2265*

and dated

From _____ *10/24/94* To _____ *12/16/95*

Inside the cover of the register, you will find a Deposit Record. Deposits may be recorded here as a separate record of how much money goes into the Sharechek account. This record is not essential since all deposits must be recorded in the register itself.

It is important to always write down all deposits and withdrawals in your register. This enables you to know how much money you have in your checking account today—even though you may have made deposits and written checks since receiving your last statement.

When writing checks, record in your register the:
1) Check number.
2) Date of the check.
3) Payee (to whom you made out the check).
4) Purpose of the check (and if it is tax-deductible).
5) Amount of the check. When you write a check or make an ATM withdrawal, subtract the amount of the withdrawal from the previous balance and write in the new balance.

When making deposits, record in your register the:
- Date of the deposit.
- Source or description of the deposit.
- Amount of the deposit. Add the amount of the deposit to the previous balance and write in the new balance.

Always make an entry in your register at the time you write a Sharechek, deposit or transfer funds, or make an ATM transaction affecting your Sharechek account balance.

	SHARECHEK REGISTER		A			
		BALANCE FORWARD	√	876	09	
1	NO. 2158 TO 3 *Food City*	DEPOSIT (+) SHARECHEK(−)	√	−138	00	}5
2	DATE 4/2 FOR 4 *Groceries* 4 ☐ TAX ITEM	BALANCE		738	09	
	NO. 2159 TO *Hudson's Dept. Store*	DEPOSIT (+) SHARECHEK(−)	√	−76	81	
	DATE 4/2 FOR *Clothes for Kids* ☐ TAX ITEM	BALANCE		661	28	
	NO. 2160 TO *Diamond's Dept. Store*	DEPOSIT (+) SHARECHEK(−)		−45	00	G
	DATE 4/4 FOR *Charge Card payment* ☐ TAX ITEM	BALANCE		616	28	
	NO. 2161 TO *May's Jewelers*	DEPOSIT (+) SHARECHEK(−)	√	−49	00	
	DATE 4/8 FOR *Layaway payment* ☐ TAX ITEM	BALANCE		567	28	
	NO. ATM TO *Transfer from*	DEPOSIT (+) SHARECHEK(−)	√	+100	00	
	DATE 4/9 FOR *Share Savings* ☐ TAX ITEM	BALANCE		667	28	

Balancing your Sharechek account

Balancing (or reconciling) your Sharechek account is the process you should follow each month when you receive your statement. The process consists of:

- Comparing your Sharechek register with the "Sharechek Account" and "Sharecheks Presented" sections of your statement.
- Making necessary entries in your register to bring it into agreement with your statement as of the statement date.

How To Reconcile Your Sharechek Account

Verify the amount of each item on the Sharechek Account portion of your statement with the amount entered in your register.

1. ENTER Register Balance ....$ B 804 53

2. Enter here, **ADD** and check off in your register, items from "Sharechek Account" portion of statement not entered in your register:

- Sharechek Deposits ....+_____|__

- Transfers to Sharechek ....+_____|__
  (including LOC advances, if any)

- Dividends ....+ C 86

- Credit Adjustments +_____|__

3. SUBTOTAL (Lines 1+2) .$ 805 39

4. Enter here and **SUBTRACT**, then check off in your register, items from "Sharechek Account" portion of statement not entered in your register.

- Any Charges/Fees ...- E 7 50

- Minus Adjustments.-_____|__

- Transfers/ATM Withdrawals from Sharechek ....-_____|__
  (including automatic LOC payments, if any)

ADJUSTED REGISTER BALANCE*(Lines 3-4) .....$ F 797 89

5. LIST and **TOTAL** Sharecheks, ATM withdrawals and transfers from Sharechek account shown in your register but NOT listed on your statement:

No.	Date	Amount	
2160	4-4	G	45 00
2162	4-12	G	12 75

(Continue, next column, top...)

No.	Date	Amount

6. SUBTOTAL ....$ H 57 75

7. ENTER ending balance from statement ....$ I 655 64

8. ADD share purchases, ATM deposits and transfers to Sharechek not on statement ....+ J 200 00

......................................+_____|__

9. SUBTOTAL (Lines 7+8)....$ K 855 64

10. SUBTRACT SUBTOTAL (Line 6)..........................- L 57 75

ADJUSTED STATEMENT BALANCE* ....$ M 797 89

*NOTE: The adjusted register and statement balances should agree.

Courtesy of Navy Federal Credit Union

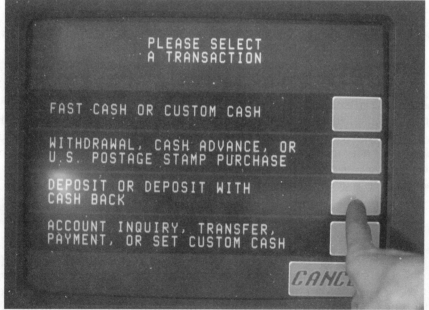

Improvements in ATM technology from Bay Bank, for example, mean that customer screens have filters that keep onlookers from seeing a customer's screen information. Also, customers can get 30-day statements for checking accounts, make loan payments electronically, and get information on loan payments and due dates.

ATM SAFETY TIPS

- Memorize your Personal Information Number (PIN). Don't write it on your ATM card or tell it to anyone else.

- Don't give your ATM card to anyone.

- Keep your ATM card from getting scratched, exposed to heat or sunlight, or exposed to anything magnetized.

- Watch your surroundings when you use an ATM and avoid machines where there's no lighting or where anyone suspicious is nearby.

- Be ready with your card and any paperwork when you step up to the machine.

- Take your receipt.

- Stand squarely in front of the machine to keep others from seeing you enter your PIN.

- Report lost or stolen ATM cards to your bank or credit union immediately.

Source: NYCE and PLUS bank machine networks

If you can join a credit union, it's advisable to do so. You never know when you could use the membership benefits, such as loans with less expensive interest rates than typical banks. Whether you'll put your checking account there is another question that goes back to convenience and ease of use. Many credit unions are smaller institutions and may not have their own automated teller machines, for example. They may have other ways you can get cash quickly, but it's in your best interest to see what they offer and if it meets your checking needs.

Using the Account

If your workplace offers direct deposit, which routes the money directly from your employer into your checking account, take it. You'll get a paystub and receipt that substitutes for your check, so you're assured you've got the necessary copies of your payroll information. But you won't have to bother going to the bank or waiting in line at an ATM machine to make a deposit. This way is safe and saves time. The Social Security Administration likes the system so much it is now using direct deposit to get money into the bank accounts of senior citizens who have started drawing benefits recently. Not only does it save the Social Security Administration administrative costs, they figure that with direct deposit, your elderly grandparents are safer from purse snatchers. Also, they won't misplace their Social Security checks or forget to deposit them if the chore is handled for them.

Another benefit of direct deposit is that it may get you cheaper checking. Some banks cut their fees to customers that use direct deposit, because it means steady business for the bank and less paperwork.

A great idea to promote savings is to get your paycheck directly deposited, and then to have some of the money automatically channeled into a separate savings account. If you're not physically handling the money, you're less likely to spend it before you get it into a liquid savings or emergency fund. Technology makes it easier to comply with that old adage: Pay yourself first.

Getting the money out of the checking account to pay everyone else is the other big traffic consideration. Naturally, writing a check is the time-honored method. But with technology, other ways are cropping up:

- Paying by touch-tone telephone, which alerts the bank to take certain amounts out of your account and direct them electronically to designated vendors, such as utility companies.

- Paying by automatic deductions from checking to designated vendors, which may be your car loan lender, a health club, or an insurance company. You pick the day the deduction occurs, and manage it so that there's enough money in the account to cover the payment.

- Paying by debit card, that plastic card that looks just like a major credit card but actually takes the money out of your checking account immediately and routes it to the supermarket, or whatever store you're shopping at.

- Banking from your home computer. To accomplish this, you have to install a program like Quicken or Microsoft Money that helps you track your expenses and keep your checkbook register on a computer program. Banking by computer is an option, generally available for a monthly fee, that lets you communicate with your bank from a modem. Using this method you can arrange automatic payments to vendors.

Oops! What Did I Do Wrong?

Paying careful, regular attention to your account, along with the help of a calculator, should keep you in steady fiscal waters and spare you the grief of writing checks for more than you have in your account. Not only will you be embarrassed if you bounce a check, you'll likely get hit with a fee from the bank, and be asked by the check recipient to cover the fee they were assessed by the bank. Yes, banks charge fees to unwitting souls or business owners who try to deposit a check only to have it bounce.

According to the staff at the Navy Federal Credit Union, based in Vienna, Virginia, many checking account errors can be traced to one of the following mistakes. The credit union is used to serving young adults managing their military pay as their first job. As the biggest credit union in the world, it sees lots of customers in this category, and sometimes helps customers balance their checkbooks, or gives them guidance with problems they've run into with other institutions. Here are the most common pitfalls:

- Writing a check and forgetting to record it in the register so that you don't deduct the amount from your account. Sometimes you can call an institution and get this information from them.

- Not keeping the register balanced in general, by recording all deposits, ATM transactions, and so forth.

- Bad timing, as in writing checks a couple of days before you'll be making a deposit, and hoping the deposit catches up in time to cover the checks. Funds move quickly nowadays, and you can bounce a check this way. Direct deposit helps because the paycheck is in your account so quickly. Otherwise, find out from your bank when the money from checks you deposit is available for use. The answer may differ according to whether the check is from a big local company or from your cousin two states away.

- Having two people write checks from a joint account, but not getting all the checks recorded in the register and deducted. It's easy to slip this way because only one person has the register and the other forgets to tell them about the new bookkeeping. There are several ways to handle this (more on that a little later in this chapter).

- Letting some fees go unaccounted for, ATM fees, for example, or using services without checking on any fees that might apply.

- Letting the micro-encoded numbers on the bottom of your check, which include your account number, fall into the wrong hands. Fraud artists can take your numbers to produce fake checks on your account. They steal money by using or cashing these bogus checks. If a company wants a blank check of yours to establish electronic withdrawals on your account for some service, for example, and the company seems at all suspect to you, don't provide the check or account numbers.

- Making too many transfers from savings to checking in a month, usually by ATM. Some people do this to get a higher interest rate offered on savings accounts, and pump the money into checking only when they need to cover bills. But federal regulation limits consumers to six of these transfers a month, so if you're making seven or more for bill paying, your checks can bounce.

- Ignoring monthly statements; these statements could help you find a mistake, something you overlooked, or suspicious activity by a thief.

- Misunderstanding what you need to do to stop automatic drafts to a vendor like a health club. You have to cancel the contract with the company receiving the money, as well as telling the bank to stop payments from the bank. Don't expect that telling the bank alone will solve the problem, because the contract with your vendor takes precedence. The upshot is you could be paying for a month or more than you intended.

Besides generally managing your account to avoid such problems, you can provide yourself with a safety net: overdraft protection. That's a feature where your bank lends you money—charging interest—to cover your checks if you're overdrawn. You have to qualify for the credit, and realize there's a limit set on how much the institution will lend you. You're not likely to hit the limit all at once. Check the terms on how the bank covers overdrafts. It may supply money in increments of hundreds, for example, even if that's more than you need to cover the check. And of course, you have to repay the bank. Overdraft protection is a hedge against unusual problems that may crop up. It's not a tool for monthly checkbook management. Another alternative is to see whether money from a savings account can be transferred to checking to cover any shortfalls.

Special Situations: Couples

If you're married, living with someone, or have a joint checking account with another person for some other reason, you've got to be more careful about your record keeping than if you were flying solo. Not only do you have to be careful to record all checks written, you have to remember ATM transactions and deposits and tell your partner about them if he or she has the checkbook register. Some people find this works fine without any difficulty: Either they are careful and communicative enough, or only one person actually uses the checkbook. The other one might get cash from the checkbook holder or use credit cards. The big financial benefit to having one checkbook is that it means paying for only one checking account. Emotionally, some people may feel it's more appropriate to pool their resources in one account as an important part of sharing.

But that's not the only way to go, especially if you are prone to bookkeeping errors, or can't remember to bring all your ATM slips home. In that case, two partners might each have their own checking accounts, and be responsible for different bills, or for portions of bills. This too, requires communication and coordination. It may be time-consuming to have two people so involved in billpaying, but the advantage is that both parties get a realistic grasp of what it takes to run the household.

A third method may be for each party to have their own checking accounts for personal expenses, spending money, or gifts for each other, and then to direct money from those accounts into a third household account meant specifically for bill paying. This account could be either an individual or joint account. The reason for going this way might be that one person could handle the bills instead of involving both parties. Even so, both people in the couple would have the chance to trade "checkbook duty" from time to time. That arrangement would keep one person from being burdened all the time, and would still give both parties a financial glimpse of the household. Still, the couple would need good communication to come to a workable arrangement, just as with the other methods.

Special Situations: Businesses

If you're starting a business with any regular income and bills, accountants generally advise getting a separate checking account for the business. There's an added expense, but that way you get all your expenses recorded correctly instead of mixed up with the household accounts. It's important to keep your business deductions recorded so that you can figure the right profit or loss on the business, and not end up paying too much in taxes.

If you're starting something smaller on the side, say a home-based business that's not very complex to run, you might still want a separate checking account with low activity. Some people do handle all such businesses inside their regular checking accounts, but they have to be careful to make sure they track the checkbook register for any tax deductions for their businesses, or for income.

Safety Sense

What if you lost your wallet, or checkbook, or both? Would you know where to start to protect your bank accounts or wallet contents?

First, let's start with the wallet. Credit card companies have a handy service they offer for an annual fee, called a credit card registry. You provide them a detailed list of everything in your wallet, from credit cards to membership cards. If something happens to your wallet, you call the registry, and they start calling all the businesses and credit card companies to let them know you need new cards. The general policy is to cancel the old card and issue you one with a new number. This prevents you from getting saddled with any charges if a thief gets your credit card and starts charging away on it and forging your signature. Of course, you have to keep the registry updated, and you have to keep the number of the registry at home in a separate spot.

Another approach would be to create your own credit card registry at home. Record the contents of your wallet, and write down the account number and the emergency customer service contact number. It might be on the card, or should be on any material the company sent you, such as a bill or brochure.

And, as the banks tell you: Don't put the personal identification number (PIN) you need for your ATM or other cards in your wallet. That makes it easy for thieves to get at your money. Instead, use PINs that you can easily remember.

With your checkbook, you'll need to contact the checking institution and get their advice. They also might advise closing the account and starting a new one.

Action Items

Arrange a regular time in your schedule and a regular place to handle your bookkeeping and checking account functions. Don't overlook these chores until the last minute or handle them when you're tired. Put the bills in a regular place until you're ready to deal with them, instead of setting them down in various places in your home.

Start a filing system to keep your bills, warranties, wallet information, and banking paperwork in order, just as you have with your paystubs. Even if you don't have much room in your home for a file cabinet, you can buy a plastic file box at a discount store that will serve the same purpose.

Keep your eye out for the best deals in banking services: Several reputable commercial companies can provide you with checks cheaper than banks, for example. Watch newspaper articles for surveys on prices banks charge for services so you can comparison shop.

CASE IN POINT:

Easy, Economical Checking

Let's say we have a 23-year-old employee named Michelle who is working in her first full-time job in an engineering company. She's no longer eligible for the student checking she had in college, but she finds a bank—or maybe a credit union through work—that offers a good deal on checking.

Michelle arranges direct deposit of her paycheck every Friday morning, and this way she gets free checking.

She has her monthly car loan payment automatically deducted from her checking account on the 15th of every month, and this gives her a break on the interest rate. Also, she has $25 switched from her checking account each Friday to savings, so she can build up some money for investing.

Michelle already took $1,000 she had saved and put it in a money market account. That's her emergency fund in case of job loss or some unforeseen disaster.

Michelle orders her checks from a printing company instead of the bank; that way she gets a better deal.

She's careful not to make too many trips to the ATM machine in a month so that she doesn't incur a charge.

She keeps her checkbook up to date and spends time reconciling the account to her statement one of the two times a month she sits down with her bills.

In case there's some sort of mistake, she applies for overdraft protection so she doesn't bounce any checks. This is a credit line, but as her savings grow, she may switch this coverage to her savings line to stay away from unnecessary debt.

Chapter 4

Spending Plans You Can Live With

Budgets can make a lot of people
nervous. Somehow, the phrases "making a budget" and "sticking to a budget" have
taken on a punitive feel. People feel that a budget—read deprivation—is the justice
being exacted for unwise spending, overspending, or simply working at a job—maybe
more than one—that doesn't pay very much.

Here's where we run into some twisted, if common, thinking. The unfortunate outcomes of unwise spending or overspending are that you may have less money for the
things most important to you and that you may pay your bills late and rack up interest
charges or late fees. And the result of working at a job that doesn't pay very well is that
you have less money to spend than some of your contemporaries. In either case, you
want to make adjustments. The conditions that lead you to budget may be unpleasant,
but the budget itself isn't. A budget is just the tool you need when money is tight.

In any financial circumstance, from loaded to drained, it makes sense to have a formula for how you'll use your resources—money—to buy food, shelter, clothing, and
other items. If you just left such matters to chance, even if you had lots of cash, you'd

likely end up spending more on some basics than you wanted and less on others. Budgets reflect choices and tastes as well as unadorned numbers. So think of this formula as a spending plan if that sounds more palatable to you than the word "budget." The most important thing is to start viewing your purchases as events that often can be anticipated and handled without panic or surprise. When you look at it that way, you realize that planning your spending doesn't cause stress, it relieves it.

Of course, plans can be changed and amended as conditions change. Naturally, if you get a raise, or move to a less expensive area, you can make changes to your plan. If, in a year's time, you run into new expenses like increased housing prices, revisit your plan to see where the money will come from. Maybe you'll subsidize a rent increase by riding a bike and lowering your transportation costs. Perhaps instead, you'll substitute your current housing situation for a different one, a less expensive place, or a roommate. Or maybe you'll choose to earn more income through another job or overtime shifts. Plans aren't cast in stone. They're works in progress, just like your financial life.

Getting Started

Now that you're well informed about how to read your paystub, and the best way to get cash into your checking account, it should be easy to figure out how much money you're going to have to work with. You'll look at the stubs or the deposit slips for a month for your starting point. This assumes that you get regular pay. If you work seasonally, are subject to layoff, or do temp work, your situation is more complicated. In that case, it's probably safest to start by figuring out what the base, or minimum, monthly income you'll have is. In some cases, this is going to take some discipline, especially if you work seasonally, and have to save your earnings to spend over several months. But if you had summer jobs to create cash flow for your months in college, you've already got some experience with this.

Using a Model

On pages 40 and 41 there is a model expense plan put out by the National Foundation for Consumer Credit. This isn't the only worksheet of its kind. Others are available in hard copy from financial institutions, and several computer programs like Quicken offer models to follow or customize as well.

This worksheet in particular, though, has several advantages that really help with the planning process, and that you could you use as examples in your own situation.

1. The time elements for both expenses and income are weekly, monthly, quarterly, and yearly. These time elements let a person take into account events that are oddly timed, but do definitely recur. Maybe your auto insurance is billed three times a year, for example. Knowing that, a good way to handle the payments for that expense is to account for some money weekly so the bill doesn't catch you by surprise. Some income can be inconsistent, too, such as extra jobs that happen

only in the summer or during holiday season, or a year-end bonus. The great thing about plotting these events against your expenses is that this shows you how much money you need to earn to meet your desired expenses. That's a lot better than having the expenses and then just hoping any extra money that's required comes along.

2. That works right in with the goals column on the far right. True, you may not have an actual objective for every line item, as you might for savings (a great line item to include in a plan), but jot down your thoughts for ones you could change: Increase payments on your credit card balance by 10 percent, buy a new suit for work and budget that into your clothing allowance, or switch to a generic pre- scription and compute the savings in your health expenditures. This type of tin- kering will lead you to clearer action steps than you would have taken otherwise.

3. Another thing that's handy about this worksheet is that it shows you the true expense of having or operating something in one lump sum. Under the headings "Shelter" and "Transportation," for example, you'll see that insurance and mainte- nance lines are included. This is more realistic than some budgets that break out all kinds of insurance as a separate category, apart from housing or car payments, for example. Sound like a small point? Not really. That's because looking only at a rent amount or a car payment will only give you part of the picture—granted a big part, but not the whole—of what it costs to live in a certain neighborhood or drive a certain kind of car. Car insurance rates, in part, depend on the kind of car being driven and the area in which you live.

4. After you understand how much it costs to maintain certain lifestyle items, you can go back to the time element first discussed, and compare how long—how many hours, weeks, or months—it takes you to earn enough money to afford a given item. You can use this with big-ticket items as well as smaller expenses. Say you earn $9 an hour and you spend $5.50 to eat your lunch at a fast-food place. Sure, fast-food places are cheaper than some other options, but you're still spend- ing $5.50. Did you really want to part with more than half your gross earnings for an hour on a quick meal? Brownbagging starts looking more attractive. How much work does it take to cover your monthly utility or phone bills? What about a new coat, or an increase in housing costs? When the relationship between time spent earning money and the costs of items emerges more clearly in your mind, you'll have a firmer grasp of what items truly have the most value to you.

5. The highly detailed line items—including snacks, cosmetics, and gifts—help you to see the spending picture accurately. Many times, people are spending money on these items and don't realize it. They can't think where their "walking around" money goes. If you want to economize, these are natural categories to consider, but you've got to know what you're doing first. Lots of people advise keeping a log of all your expenditures in a notebook for a month. You can combine that exercise with this worksheet and get the benefit of the most accurate data possible.

WORKSHEET**

EXPENSES	Weekly	Monthly	Quarterly	Yearly	Goals
Shelter					
Mortgage or Rent					
Utilities: Heat					
Electric					
Garbage/Sewer/Water					
Telephone					
Property Taxes*					
Insurance*					
Furnishings					
Maintenance*					
Assoc. Dues/Condos					
Transportation					
Car Payment/Lease					
Car Payment/Lease					
Insurance*					
License/Registration*					
Maintenance*					
Gasoline					
Parking/Tolls/Taxi/Bus					
Food					
Groceries					
Lunches/Snacks					
Health					
Insurance*					
Doctor(s)*					
Dentist*					
Prescription Drugs*					
Clothes					
Purchases					
Cleaning/Laundry					
Personal					
Haircuts/Cosmetics					
Alcohol/Tobacco					
Other					
Entertainment					
Dining Out					
Cable/Videos/Movies					
Magazines/Newspapers					
Vacations					
Other					

*These expenses occur on an irregular basis; money must be set aside on a weekly or monthly basis to meet them.

**Only consider net income and enter expenses, not money already withheld from paycheck.

WORKSHEET** (Continued)

Education				
Tuition & Fees*				
School Supplies				
Books				
Savings				
Financial Institution				
Company Savings Plan				
IRA				
Other				
Family Needs				
Life Insurance*				
Child Care				
Child Support				
Pets				
Allowances/Gifts				
Additional Items				
Donations				
Membership Dues*				
Taxes (Not Already Withheld)*				
Other				
Credit Payments				
Credit Card				
Credit Card				
Credit Card				
Department Store				
Gasoline Card				
Student Loan				
Other				
TOTAL EXPENSES				
INCOME				
Paycheck				
Paycheck				
Gratuities				
Dividends/Interest				
Pension/Social Security				
Child Support				
Gifts				
TOTAL INCOME				

*These expenses occur on an irregular basis; money must be set aside on a weekly or monthly basis to meet them.

**Only consider net income and enter expenses, not money already withheld from paycheck.

Living with the Plan

Drawing up a budget is one big step, following it is another. You're going to have to allow yourself—and your partner, if you have one— some flexibility on this, some allowances for errors, inexperience, or simply the unintended. As you build up your savings and an emergency fund, such surprises won't be so painful because you'll have a way to cover them.

In the meantime, here are some things to consider as you work with your plan:

- Lots of advisers recommend having an emergency fund of three to six months' worth of living expenses in case you lose your job.

- It's easier to save if you "pay yourself first."

- Time is money, as the saying goes. Consider carefully any time-saving conveniences. Processed foods can cost more, for example. On the other hand, it may be worth it to pay for an item or service if you lack the expertise to do it well, or if you can spend the time earning more money for yourself using your skills and talents. If you pay someone to do your resume more professionally and impressively than you could have managed on your own, and the finished product gets you a better job, the outlay may have been worth the investment.

- Plan to spend money and time on yourself for fun, because if you don't, you may rebel and blow your whole plan. Think of it this way: Just as diets tend to promote binges, deprivation can eventually trigger financial intemperance. Moderation makes the most sense—psychologically and fiscally. Just remember that lots of entertainment is inexpensive—community events and rented or borrowed videotapes, for example—and it may be the time you spend relaxing that's so crucial to your well-being, not attending the most hyped or expensive events around.

TIDBIT: There's a lot of budgeting help around. Besides books and computer programs, the Consumer Credit Counseling Service can be reached at 1-800-388-2227. Member offices report that 35 percent of consumers who contact them are able to help themselves after they get a budget counseling session. Or, check out the NFCC home page at http://www.nfcc.org, or look for classes or workshops at adult education programs, work, banks, or credit unions. Websurfers also might try out the American Bankers Association home page's interactive personal finance section at http://www.aba.com.

Getting Through an Emergency

Say you've done everything you can, and you've started an emergency fund, but the engine on your car just blew. You don't yet have the several hundred dollars it will take to make the repair, and you need the car to get to work. You feel like budgets and spending plans are fine after you've had the chance to earn money for a longer period, but what do you do in this circumstance? Judy Lau, a certified financial planner, has some suggestions. Lau is president of Lau & Associates in Wilmington, Delaware. Rather than resorting immediately to a credit card (more on that in Chapter 6), Lau recommends trying one of these options, in order of their desirability:

1. See if you can work out a payment plan with the mechanic, or the vendor of whatever service is needed in your particular case.

2. Ask your family to lend you the money with a proposed repayment plan and "Have it in writing." Your folks may be called on to bail you out again. You need to have a good credit reputation with them.

3. If you have an understanding or flexible employer, ask if there's a policy that would let you have an interest-free loan or cash advance that you might repay through paycheck deductions.

4. Take the hit on a credit card and plan to repay the interest and balance as promptly as possible.

5. If you have any hard assets like mutual funds, sell them to pay the expense, but realize you might incur tax in doing so: a capital gains tax that is levied on the profits.

Like other prudent financial advisers, Lau recommends that young people trim back on some expenses and come up with a savings cushion so that these kinds of instances don't happen too often.

Doing Good in Your Budget

Often, people feel that once they start making a livable, steady income, they'd like to support some of their favorite causes. Most charities solicit all year round, and some especially look for donations around the holiday season. A natural disaster or local emergency can strike at any time, and you may want to make a contribution.

How do you handle these events? The unexpected events when people or agencies need cash are harder to budget for. They fall under your miscellaneous items in most budgets.

But some people do budget to include their favorite charities, whether it's a place of worship to which they give weekly, or an annual donation to a favorite cause.

TIDBIT: A study by the Independent Sector found that college graduates, as a group, contributed 2.8 percent of their household income to charity in 1995. People up to age 24 gave 0.6 percent of their income, and those aged 25 to 34 gave 1.6 percent of their income.

It's more difficult when you're first starting out, but a consortium of nonprofits called Independent Sector has come up with some guidelines for charitable giving. Independent Sector's slogan for people is to "Give Five"—meaning volunteering five hours a week to nonprofit causes you care about and by giving 5 percent of your household income to charity. You can consider this a goal you might work toward eventually and do what you can in the meantime.

GUIDELINES FOR CONTRIBUTORS

- Budget for giving.

- Keep track of pledges you've made so you can follow up on promises to pay.

- Ask if your employer offers any matching-funds programs for employee gifts to charity.

- If you get a phone call or visit at home, get the solicitor's name, the name of the organization, and the activities for which the money is being raised.

- Before you buy goods or tickets or the like, find out the name of the organization. If the organization isn't familiar to you, find out if they have any written material and how much of the price of your ticket or purchase will actually go to the organization.

- Watch out for any solicitations that are high pressure.

- If you don't know an organization, ask for written material on it, such as its annual report.

- Favor the causes that spend the most on programs as opposed to overhead.

- If you want your contribution to be anonymous, tell the organization.

- Get a receipt for possible tax deductions, especially for contributions of $250 or more made in a single payment.

- If you have property that you might someday consider donating to charity or leaving to charity in a will, ask an attorney or accountant for help.

GUIDELINES FOR VOLUNTEERS

- Know what you want to get out of volunteering, whether it's to support a cause, meet new friends, or both, so you can make a good selection.

- Ask yourself whether the time commitment fits your lifestyle.

- Think about what skills you have that could be used in a volunteer setting.

- Check to see if your employer has any company volunteer programs or referral services.

- Watch for volunteer opportunities when you're at arts and civic events, hospitals, schools, religious settings, and churches.

- Talk to the director of volunteers about training, hours, supervision, and expectations.

- Be honest about what kinds of work you find meaningful and satisfying.

- Give and take feedback, and suggest changes where appropriate.

- Respect confidentiality in volunteer settings.

- Have a giving heart and a sense of humor.

Source: Adapted from the Independent Sector Guidelines

When you're just starting out in your career, you may find it easier to volunteer time (rather than money), especially if you're single and have few other commitments besides work. You may find volunteer options through your workplace, through charitable functions of your field of endeavor, through community or religious affiliations, through social causes, hobbies, or just in the neighborhood or in the newspaper. Independent Sector points out that people often have to juggle their schedules so five hours might be accomplished during lunch hours, or on two Saturdays a month, or whenever you can fit it in. You also might consider that five hours teaching someone to read or cleaning up a river or roadside makes for five hours you can't spend wandering around a shopping mall or frittering away on other activities that might cost you money.

When you decide to donate money, Independent Sector advises that you look at causes where you already give some time. Local United Way and Better Business Bureaus also have information on charities operating in particular areas. And because there are so many charities competing for the same dollars, and sometimes several causes in one field of interest, the media often look at where your dollars could do the most good. For example, an environmental magazine may write about which ecologically oriented groups seem to be the most effective. Many media look at how well charities use the money that is given to them. For example, the November 1996 issue of *Money* magazine looked at the nation's 25 biggest charities and decided the American Red Cross was the best run because, among other reasons, it was able to spend 91.5 percent of the money it takes in on programs that actually provide relief to people, and only 8.5 percent of its funds on administrative expenses like office rents, telephone lines, and so on. *Money* pointed out that the average spent on programs for the biggest charities is 78.4 percent.

That's a key point to look at: How much money actually goes to the cause for which the group was founded, as opposed to overhead? To be fair, sometimes it's harder for younger charities to achieve this same level of operational efficiency in their early years. Media often use the information supplied by organizations that review charities, the National Charities Information Bureau (http://www.give.org). On the World Wide Web, you can also find a Nonprofit Website Directory (http://www.contact.org) and the Internet Nonprofit Center (http.//www.nonprofits.org), which can help you find out if charities are for real, and what they do. These review agencies exist so that charities will do a better job, and so that people won't feel pressured or harassed into giving. When you're asked for money, remember, you always have the right to think about it, ask for more information, and to say no, thank you. You can get deductions on your federal income tax form for money you give to charity or mileage for volunteer efforts, but only as itemized deductions, so probably when you're starting out, your charitable giving is going to be motivated more by goodwill than tax strategy.

Independent Sector maintains that instead of spreading your charitable dollars around, it's better to channel most of your energy to the causes dearest to your heart. Independent Sector points out there are also some other ways of supporting charity, like purchasing items that donate a portion of the proceeds to charity, or buying items from nonprofit groups. It also makes sense to regularly go through your household goods and clothing and donate items that are still in good repair, but that you don't use any-more. Be careful about thinking that you will use or get to something. Think about whether you've actually touched or worn an item in the last year, and if not, consider what good it might do someone else.

Action Items

Coordinate your budget documents with your bills and financial records, so that when you get a price increase or decrease on a service or utility, you can adjust your budget accordingly.

....

Notice how people in your field of work live and how they manage to stretch their paychecks. See if there are any tips you can pick up.

....

Check your company's benefits and compensation policy to make sure you're getting as much tax-free cash com-pensation as you can, and using your other benefits to their fullest, given your lifestyle and needs. For example, check on any discounts that may be offered to your employee group.

....

Check to make sure you've got the right banking accounts and bill paying format to best complement your spend-ing plan.

....

Use your budget goals as a springboard to start developing short-term, medium-term, and long-term goals. Write them down and put them in a place where you will see them regularly. This will help you stick to your plan and note the milestones you reach on the way to your goals.

....

Look at what you need in your budget or spending plan when someone asks what you'd like for a holiday or birth-day gift.

....

While you're doing this planning, plan for two other "what-if" situations. Who would sign your bills and take care of legal and financial matters if you were sick for awhile? You need to designate someone as a power of attorney, and a lawyer can help you do that. You should also designate someone to tell doctors what to do if you're injured and can't speak for yourself. This may be called a health care proxy or document or living will, available either from a legal society, or in some cases, from hospitals.

Chapter 5

Handling Student Loans

By the time you've graduated from college, the odds are even that you've taken out a loan to finance your education. Almost 50 percent of college students use loans, according to Sallie Mae, the biggest source of funding for college loans in the country. Even if you didn't borrow to get through college, if you marry someone who did, your financial future will be affected by the handling of the repayment.

Right now, the average college graduate leaves school between $11,000 and $11,500 in debt, according to Sallie Mae. The amount may be around $14,000 by the year 2000, Sallie Mae estimates. It's common for students to take out loans without really considering how they will work out the repayments: In the face of big tuition bills, loans are often a good way to bridge the finance gap. And before you've actually begun earning a regular, full-time income from the benefit of your degree, it's difficult to project what your future money handling situation will be like.

THATCH by Jeff Shesol

Cartoonist Jeff Shesol has a little fun with the nervousness some graduates have about their student loans in this October 1996 strip.

Courtesy: Creators Syndicate

But then, you get ready to graduate, and start hearing about loan repayment schedules. Maybe your job prospects haven't solidified yet. Maybe it will take awhile for you to get established. Thousands of dollars of indebtedness and years of monthly payments can seem daunting. But remember, your student loans were an investment. Unlike loans for other things you might have purchased, your student loans financed an education, and presumably, greater earnings capability than you would have had without the degree. That's a responsible, reasonable use of borrowing, and not necessarily a cause for regret.

TIDBIT: Graduating from college still pays, according to 1993 figures from the Census Bureau. College graduates continue to earn more than high school graduates—a median annual sum of $37,000 for college graduates versus $21,000 for high school graduates—and the gap is widening. Over a lifetime, census figures estimate high school graduates are likely to earn $821,000 compared to the $1,421,000 their college-educated counterparts will earn. Those with masters degrees will earn even more, $1,619,000, and professionals like doctors and lawyers may earn more than $3 million.

Failing to repay your student loans, on the other hand, would be a reason for weeping. Not repaying your loans makes it harder for you to borrow money in the future for a house, car, or other purpose. And it could mean you'd be subjected to embarrassing events like having your loan repayment deducted from your paycheck, or having any income tax refunds you thought you were getting seized. Such dire outcomes need never occur, however. There are many options for loan repayment that may help you in your current and future circumstances. Down the road, you may even be looking at a time when you can pay off the balance of your debt in a single sum, or a prepayment. In the meantime, these are the general options with federally sponsored student loan programs.

Standard Repayments

The simplest option for repaying a loan is agreeing to pay a standard sum every month for a period of years. If you have a loan with a variable interest rate, the payments can fluctuate to match the market, but you're working from the general assumption that your payments will be roughly similar over the course of the loan repayment. For instance, a government brochure uses the example of a graduate who borrows $10,000. The graduate decides to repay over 10 years: payments of $122.65. Given interest on the loan of 8.25 percent, the borrower actually repays $14,718—$4,718 for interest. That's a straightforward solution to the debt situation. But there are other options that may better fit differing circumstances. Ask your lender about these or similar programs.

Payments Based on Income

The idea here is to make the payments proportionate to what you're earning. Sallie Mae uses the example of someone earning $20,000—he or she decides how much gross monthly income between 4 percent and 25 percent will be budgeted for student loan repayment. So, if you owe $10,000 at an interest rate of 8.25 percent, in the first year you might make payments at 4 percent of your income, or $69 a month. The monthly payments might increase to $123 a month in years two through 11 of loan repayment. Note that you've gone a year longer with this arrangement than with the standard repayment plan. Going this route can make sense if you're looking at a field with low-paying entry-level jobs, but the prospect of greater earnings potential later. But be aware that this can prolong your indebtedness and your financing costs.

Graduated Payments

This is another variation for people who may need help making ends meet in their early working years. Payments aren't based on income, but are smaller in the early years of the loan, and then grow. Sallie Mae, for example, will let a borrower pay only interest for a couple of years, and then pay back interest and principal. Going this way will increase your overall interest payments over the years, but if low entry-level pay and comparatively high rents mean you can only pay $70 monthly, instead of more than $120, it makes sense to go for the option that you can dependably manage.

Switching Around

Whatever you select, you're not stuck with one option for the life of your loan repayment. You may be able to move between repayment plans as your circumstances change. In cases of hardship, including unemployment, you may get permission to defer payments for awhile, or perhaps reduce them. You need to complete a form to get a formal deferment, which you get from the outfit that is servicing your loan. If you think you need this, act as quickly as possible. It can take a month or more to process your request, and you're responsible for timely payments until alternative arrangements are agreed on.

Consolidating Loans

If you've got a loan from more than one source, it might make sense to bundle the loans together so that you'll have only one repayment to contend with. You may also extend the life of the loan repayment, but this will cost more over the long haul. In tight circumstances, consolidating loans may make life easier. You can count on handling only one monthly payment, and rest assured that you're taking care of your obligations.

Consolidating for Married Couples

Sallie Mae allows married couples to combine a husband's and wife's student loan obligations into one account for repayment. The same type of logic and circumstances apply: The single monthly payment makes budgeting easier, although the overall life of the loan could be extended and financing costs could be higher.

Working With the Repayment Officials

It's going to be important to know what institution is servicing your loan: It might not be the same place from which you originally borrowed the money. Sallie Mae, for example, buys student loans and then handles the servicing of borrowers, collecting the money and keeping the records.

When you talk to a lender or loan servicing company over the phone, make sure you keep accurate and detailed notes of all your conversations. Likewise, keep copies of any correspondence. Make sure you keep them abreast of any changes in your address.

Similarly, pay attention to any mailings you get from these folks to stay informed of changes in the ownership or servicing of your loan. Have any toll-free customer service numbers in your files in case you have any questions. Be on the lookout for any ways of handling loan repayments that will make the process easier or less expensive: Automatic deductions from bank accounts might ease the paperwork and earn you a discount on the interest.

Financing Graduate School

Undergraduate loans can be a challenge for some people, but they are often manageable. The real trials can come when someone racks up some undergraduate debt and then wants a graduate degree, also to be financed by debt. For the most part, these are the people who end up in newspaper stories about colossal debts haunting young professionals.

This is something certified financial planner Philip C. Johnson sees in his practice in Clifton Park, New York, near Albany. Debt allows people to accomplish their educational goals, Johnson agrees, so it "isn't altogether a bad thing. You just want to be able to control it so that it doesn't control you later in life." What kind of scenario is he describing?

Couples who have married in or out of graduate school may already have a child to support and may want to buy a house. Or maybe one spouse is working and the other is still in school. Those still in school can defer previous debt until graduate work is over, but eventually, they could be facing $40,000 in debt, Johnson says, "much of which is related to graduate school."

Graduate school, Johnson stresses, is a different scene financially than two- or four-year colleges. True, in some fields the advanced degree is necessary for career advancement. But for your own financial planning, you need to realize that graduate school tuition is going to be more expensive than undergraduate tuition and there may well be less aid available, depending on the field you select. That's what makes loans so much more prevalent. Yet the added degree may not give you such a big boost in earnings potential that loan repayments become easy.

What to do? If you're lucky enough to be going into a field where fellowships will pay your way, count your blessings. Otherwise, you're going to have to shop seriously for the best deals in tuition and degree value—probably even more seriously than you considered your undergraduate choice. Working and going to graduate school part-time is an option in many fields of study. You may be able to pay the tuition, or at least part of it, from current earnings, and avoid or minimize further borrowing. The best deal may be to go to work for an employer that offers tuition reimbursement for part-time study. Some employers will pay for part of the schooling, and some for all of it. It makes for a hectic and demanding schedule, and you may be tying up money until your employer repays you for the tuition fees. You may also find the employer will expect some guarantee of service in return for the tuition benefit, or that you can't afford to leave a place you don't much like because of the tuition benefits. You'll also need to check whether tuition benefits alter your taxable income status. It's all a balancing act that could require sacrifice, discipline, and money.

Action Items

Review your student loan debt against your current spending plan and your earnings projections for the future to find the best payment option. Call your lender or Sallie Mae at 1-800-643-0040, or visit the web site at http://www.salliemae.com.

_____

Keep track of earnings, pay trends, and raises in your field. Find out what you can do to keep enhancing your earnings potential.

_____

Even if you work at a small company, find out what tuition reimbursement plans might be offered to employees and under what terms.

Chapter 6

Consumer Credit

Between your student loans and any credit cards you may have been issued in college, you may feel you've already got a pretty good grasp about how credit operates. After all, plenty of college students have been able to get credit cards and handle the payments.

But getting a card as a student is somewhat different. Card issuers feel there's a good chance that if the student gets in trouble and can't cover the bills, his or her family may bail them out. Then the family is out of the money, not the credit card company.

In the meantime, the young person may have developed a taste for how easy it is to buy on impulse through credit. Durant Abernethy, president and chief executive officer of the National Foundation for Consumer Credit, says he worries for today's young working adults. "Because you've likely been able to get credit cards 'younger and easier' than other consumers," says Durant, "the temptation is tremendous." In their working lives, many adults find credit cards to be a two-edged sword. They can be useful tools when respected and prudently used. They can allow you flexibility to pay for something quickly, and to easily handle travel arrangements such as renting cars. They can serve as a substitute for cash, with the cardholder paying off balances in full every month, and perhaps earning credit card rebates or frequent flier miles as part of the bargain. A good track record—and there will be a track record in handling credit—will make it easier for you to get financing for a car (if you need it), a mortgage for a home, and, in some cases, to make the right impression on prospective employers who have the status to obtain credit reports. But you have to realize that it's debt—it's not a way of creating extra income, as some people unfortunately discover. It's not a means of buying things you can't afford to pay for. For example, certified financial planner Kyra Morris sometimes sees 20-somethings in her South Carolina area office who have run into credit trouble and they usually have little of lasting value to show for the expenditures. "It's usually bar stuff, clothes, travel, mostly entertainment—not even tangible items." Understanding more about the credit business will help you manage your credit resources wisely.

How Credit Is Granted

Whether it's a bank, a credit card company, an auto financing outfit, or a member of the family, most credit arrangements work according to the same general principles. You need money for a specific purpose, or access to a line of credit for a multitude of purposes, and you need the lender to make that money available. Lenders talk about "three Cs" they like to see in a borrower: *character*, *capacity*, and *collateral*.

Character means that you'll be true to your word— the borrowing contract or note—and pay back the money. Character is usually demonstrated by your history of handling bills.

Capacity means you're earning enough money to afford the payments. The lender will check your earnings and perhaps your employment history to make sure that you can keep a job, or keep earning money in your field, even if you seem to have moved from one employer to another recently.

Collateral is important in the bigger loans—it's some kind of asset that the bank knows is available to cover your loan payments if you lose your job and your cash flow stops. It might be money in a retirement account, a car, a piece of equipment, or property. Though most credit cards aren't backed up by any collateral—and so are known in the industry as unsecured credit—some cards are secured cards. The secured-card borrower has to come up with a bank deposit that cannot be touched as long as they have the card—and often for awhile after the card is canceled. The secured deposit gives the lender some collateral. Yes, this is expensive and ties up cash, but it can help someone with no credit or poor credit establish a reputable history.

In an instance where you don't have any collateral to offer and the lender requires it, you may be able to get a person with a more established credit track record to cosign the loan for you; in effect, acting as your partner. But the partner is obliged legally to repay the loan if you can't, so people don't take on this task lightly either. Sometimes you simply can't get the loan.

How to Shop for Credit

Despite all the warnings that get issued about credit, it's also true that credit has become more of a commodity in recent years than a privilege. Banks and lenders make plenty of money from the interest, annual fees, and any other charges they make letting plastic circulate. That's feasible because most people repay their loans. The companies have a constant supply of money circulating that's making more money, and that works to make more credit available to create even more profits. These companies are also competing with each other for the opportunity to get in on this business.

This means responsible and savvy borrowers should look hard at the credit card offers they get. Look for the best price and terms. Some companies may waive an annual fee if you like. Some may offer a lower rate, or a longer grace period—the amount of days after a purchase is charged before interest starts accruing. Some may use less expensive ways of calculating interest—which is based on the annual percentage rate attached to the card. That's explained in the disclosure statement that comes with the card, and shown on the statement. If it doesn't make sense to you, call the toll-free customer service line and ask a representative to explain it to you.

TIDBIT: The most common way of calculating interest refers to the average daily balance. The lender adds up your daily balances for the billing cycle, and then divides that sum by the number of days in the billing cycle. Lenders also might figure interest charges by subtracting payments from the total owed; by figuring interest on the sum the customer owed at the beginning of the billing cycle; or some variation of these methods.

Some cards may charge more, but may offer services you like and are willing to pay for, such as a credit card registry, or free travelers' checks. Comparing credit cards in this way is much like comparing banks or credit unions to see which offers the best checking package for you. Charges and conveniences are linked considerations for the buyer, but there are plenty of choices in the market. And you always can switch from one credit card to another if better terms become available from a competitive vendor.

How to Start Building Credit if You Don't Already Have It

If you're operating without a credit card, you may find it useful to have one, particularly if you're ever expected to travel for work. If you can't get qualified right away for a major credit card, which are the least expensive to have, then you'll have to take another route.

One way is to get a card with a cosigner, so you can establish a credit rating that way.

Another is to start with a card that's easier to obtain, such as a store card. The downside is, these cards typically charge higher interest rates than major credit cards, and lock you into purchases at one store if you want to get a credit rating going. One way

AT&T Universal Gold MasterCard

AT&T

Account Monthly Statement
Billing Period 08/28/96-09/27/96

Page 1 of 1

L.S. ROSS

Account Number
5401 2345 6789 1234
Charter Member
No Annual Fee for Life

Quick Reference

Minimum Payment	18.33
New Balance	732.99
Due Date	10/29/96
Credit Line	2,000.00
Available Credit	1,267.00

Calling Card
2212345678 + PIN

? AT&T Account on Call 1 800 636-8330
Customer Service 1 800 423-4343
Internet Address: www.att.com/ucs/

Previous Balance $726.89

Payments, Credits & Adjustments

Trans	Post	Description	Payments/Credits	Adjustments
09/17		Payment Received Thank You.	50.00CR	
09/16	10/16	Go Travel Jacksonville FL	75.00CR	
		1 Payment and 1 Credit		$125.00CR

Purchases

Trans	Post	Description	Charges
09/05	09/05	Harry's Diner Jacksonville FL	44.00
09/17	09/17	Shreveport Inn Amelia Island FL	75.00
		2 Transactions	$119.00

$ Cash

Your card gives you access to over 430,000 ATMs and financial institutions. $0.00

Calling Card

No.	Date	Time	Place and Number	Rate	Minutes	Amount
1	09/03	11:06 P.M.	EULESS TX 221-456-7891	N/Wknd	13	3.19
			CALLED FROM JACKSONVILLE FL 221-567-8910			
			Domestic Calls			3.19
			Card Number:221-2345678			3.19
			Total AT&T Calls			3.19
			Total Calls			3.19
			Federal Tax @ 3%			.10
			State and Local Taxes			.04
			1 Transaction through 09/27/96			$3.33

Note: calling card charges are due in full each month and are included in minimum payment.

Finance Charge Information

	Purchases	Cash Advances	Promotions
Nominal APR	17.20%	17.20%	0.00%
Daily Periodic Rate	.0471%	.0471%	.0000%
x No. of Days in Billing Cycle	31	31	31
x Average Daily Balance	$0.00	$0.00	$0.00
= Periodic *FINANCE CHARGE*	$0.00	$0.00	$0.00
+ Cash Advance Fee/*FINANCE CHARGE*		$0.00	
= Total *FINANCE CHARGE*			$0.00
Effective *ANNUAL PERCENTAGE RATE*			

New Balance

News From AT&T Universal Card

Forgot your PIN? Want to choose your own? Call us at 1 800 423-4343.

Payment Record Amount Paid:_____ Date Paid:_____ Check Number:_____

Please detach and return this coupon with your payment.

Account Number	Payment Due	New Balance	Minimum Payment	Enter Amount Enclosed
5401 2345 6789 1234	10/21/96	$732.99	$18.33	$

Just a reminder...
Your statement is now printed on both sides in order to preserve our environment and reduce paper costs. Please be sure to read both sides of your statement.

Make changes to address and phone number below:

Address		Apt./Suite
City	State	Zip
Home phone ( )	Business phone ( )	

288 40 1011 29 01 B

AT&T Universal Gold MasterCard

L.S. ROSS
123 LAKESIDE DRIVE
SPRINGFIELD, OH 12345

Make check payable to:

AT&T Universal Card
P.O. Box 84011
Columbus, GA 31908-4011

53988200404122070000015000000047616

The AT&T Universal Basic and Gold Cards came out tops in a customer satisfaction survey conducted in 1996 among more than 10,000 credit card holders by the independent research firm, J.D. Power and Associates. One of the things that set the AT&T Universal card apart from some of its competition is that customers liked the clarity of information on their bills. Finance charge information, for example, is clearly spelled out.

Art: Sample bill courtesy of AT&T Universal Card

to handle this might be to get a card that would let you buy some of the work clothes you need, pay off the balances religiously, and then switch to a major credit card as fast as you can.

Managing the Credit Cards Once You Have Them

For starters, don't have too many cards. Between department store cards and other offers, it's actually easy to get four or five credit cards. That's really not to your benefit. For one thing, they just present more of a temptation to overspend. For another, when lenders for something you really need, like a car or a house, see all those credit cards on your report, they're apt to be displeased. Even if you haven't used the credit cards, as long as the accounts remain open, they have to assume you could conceivably go out and run up debt on those accounts that might hamper your ability to repay the car or house loan.

Morris recommends that you have one functional card for business use, if necessary. If you travel for your employer and have to use a credit card and get reimbursed for your expenses, you'll may find it easier to keep a card exclusively for those items. That way, when the credit card bill comes and you have to submit an expense report to your employer, you won't have any trouble keeping the bookkeeping simple and straight-forward. In such cases, you might even ask the employer to cover any annual fees for having such a card.

Secondly, Morris says, you might have a household card for your personal expenses. There's an outside possibility that you might want to have a card for gasoline expenses, which would make three. That's plenty for most people.

The best way to handle the cards is charge only items you know you can pay off at the end of the billing cycle—keeping your balance at zero. If that's not possible, at least try to make more than the minimum payment. If you only pay the minimum, interest charges (that may be 18 percent) will just keep accruing, and you'll end up paying far more than you originally intended. And if you keep charging items, you may be in perpetual debt. Consumer group Bankcard Holders of America devised this illustration to show how much time it would take, and how much it would really cost, if you repaid credit card debt only by paying the minimum required each month.

AMOUNT OWED	TIME NEEDED	INTEREST CHARGED AT 17% APR
$1,000	12 years	$979
$5,000	24$^{1}/_{3}$ years	$6,210
$10,000	29 years	$12,745

To look at it another way, if you're 24 now, and have $5,000 in credit card debt, paying only the minimum would require payments for as much time as you've already lived.

Also, be aware of the fact that you can be charged with penalties or higher interest rates for paying late or for going over your credit limit.

Commonsense Precautions

To protect yourself against credit card fraud—other people using your credit card number without your knowledge—you'll have to practice some routine precautions. Don't leave your account number lying around where other people can see it, for example, and shred any paper that has your card number on it before discarding the paper. Don't print your credit card number on the outside of correspondence, and don't give out your number over the phone unless you place the call, such as calling a catalog company. Double-check your receipts, and check them against statements. Call your credit card company right away if your statement is wrong. Also, notify the card company or your credit card registry if your card is lost or stolen. They may have to cancel your old card and issue you a new one to protect you from the financial damage the thief can create.

If you marry, it's wise for each of you to keep a credit record in your own name for a number of reasons. That way if something happens to the other person or to the relationship, each party will still have a financial history. And if one person has a good credit record and the other doesn't, blending credit into a joint record may just detract from the good history, and help neither party.

In the case of divorce, you'll need to keep any joint bills current until you can officially sever your financial ties. Then each party will have to set up individual accounts.

What About Starting a Business?

Sometimes people want to start a business in their home and need a few or even tens of thousands of dollars. Often banks don't want to consider financing these operations through their commercial divisions, because the loans cost just as much to administer as fatter agreements that will generate more interest and profits for the bank. Consequently, credit cards and credit card cash advances have filled the gap for many small business people who needed to cover the costs of some equipment, provide for their household needs while the fledgling enterprise was still too young to generate earnings, and didn't have a fat pot of savings to make it all happen.

If you're going to be building a viable business, and your investment will eventually return more income to you, Morris thinks using credit card debt is acceptable, but notes that you should have clear projections on how and when you'll pay the money back. If your earnings projections are fuzzy or pie in the sky, you may not be able to keep up with the required repayments.

Another option is get a secured credit card for your small business, which some companies are starting to market. The deposit should put a hedge between you and too much debt, and will allow the business to build some credit history.

If none of these options will work, you'll have to look for alternatives in your community. Recently, some economic developers in regional areas have started running "microloan" programs that let business people borrow enough in small amounts to get going: maybe to buy a computer or some advertising. Programs like this can help businesses being started on a shoestring and help establish good credit. They're also great for putting you in touch with other people running noncompeting businesses. You can act as a sounding board for each other on business ideas, motivate each other, and counter the isolation that sometimes develops when you're running your own business.

How to Use Your Credit Report

Credit reports are compiled from information that comes from companies with which you do business. These companies send information to clearinghouses—credit bureaus—on what kinds of financial arrangements you had with them and when you paid. It's strictly a financial document, and often contains good news, demonstrating that people paid their bills on time.

The reports are kept, generated, and updated to help future lenders decide whether to lend you money, and under what terms. The people with the best credit histories can get credit quickly, when they need it, and often at lower interest rates than consumers with less laudable records. That's why, Morris says, "a good credit rating is as valuable as a good reputation."

If you're denied a loan, you can get a credit report for free and look at your record through the lender's eyes.

Better still, it's smart to check on your credit report from time to time to see if there are any mistakes. It's also another precaution against fraud, because the report will tell you if anyone has applied for credit in your name. If you're contemplating a purchase that needs financing, it's wise to start things off by looking at your credit report and seeing first whether there is any information that needs to be cleared up. It's possible to have your name, account numbers, payment records, or other vital bits of data in error on your report. Fortunately, you can specifically dispute that information in writing to the credit bureau to get the situation rectified. Many people are nervous when they apply for a loan, and finding out that some information they weren't even aware of on their credit report is fouling up the process can be truly aggravating. Ask around at banks what credit bureaus are used in your area, then contact the bureau or bureaus to see what their policies are for providing you with your credit report, adding information, or deleting erroneous data. There are three major reporting agencies and all have toll-free numbers for consumers:

Experian (formerly TRW)	1-800-422-4879
TransUnion	1-800-916-8800
Equifax	1-800-685-1111

<u>ACCOUNT</u>	<u>DESCRIPTION</u>
1 • US BKPT CT MD 101 W LOMBART ST. BALTIMORE MD 21002 DOCKET # 08511002	VOLUNTARY BANKRUPTCY CHAPTER 13 DISCHARGED ON 05/23/92. PETITION ON 06/01/90. RECORDED ASSETS: $100,000, LIABILITIES: $8,000. YOU ARE SOLELY RESPONSIBLE FOR THIS PUBLIC RECORD ITEM.
2 • HOPKINS COUNTY COURT MADISON CNTY CT HOUSE MADISONVILLE KY 42111 DOCKET # 2005355267 BK PG SEQ # 1386520381	SMALL CLAIMS JUDGMENT SATISFIED ON 02/23/93. ORIGINAL FILING DATE 06/28/92. AMOUNT: $4,100. PLAINTIFF: WILSON AND MCPHERSON. YOU HAVE JOINT RESPONSIBILITY FOR THIS PUBLIC RECORD ITEM.
3 • LEE CO CIVIL COURT P O BOX 408 FT MYERS FL 33403 CERTIFICATE # 211412123 BK PG SEQ #	COUNTY TAX LIEN ON 12/08/91. AMOUNT: $2,000. YOU ARE SOLELY RESPONSIBLE FOR THIS PUBLIC RECORD ITEM.

This is what a sample report from Experian looks like, showing the history of the account.

While mistakes in your credit report can be rectified, accurate reporting of late payments or other unfavorable information can't be deleted. Experian points out that negative information can stay on the credit report for as many as seven years, and bankruptcy information can stay on the credit report for as many as 10 years. So only the passage of time, characterized by wise money management, can counterbalance past missteps.

What to Do if You Get Into Trouble

Outside of mortgage or rent, no more than 20 percent of your monthly income should be going to service consumer debt, warns the National Foundation for Consumer Credit. Look over your bills and income with a calculator and determine this ratio. In addition, beware of any of the following warning signs of trouble:

- Being unable to make more than the minimum payment

- Borrowing from one credit line to pay another (as opposed to replacing an expensive credit line with a less expensive credit line)

- Having trouble paying housing costs, or needing credit to buy groceries

- Being hit with penalties or increased interest rates because of late payments or mounting debt load

- Getting nervous about money or arguing about purchases with others in the household

If lenders or their collection people start calling you to ask when you'll be sending the money, which they might, day and night, no matter how unpleasant or embarrassing you find this, then there's no avoiding the conclusion that you're in too deep.

You'll want to stop using your credit cards immediately—some people even advise leaving them at home in a drawer or frozen in a block of ice in the freezer. That way you'll have time to really think about the purchase while you're retrieving the card from someplace less handy than your wallet. You'll need to look at ways that perhaps you can add extra income, and/or cut down on debt.

If you need to restructure the debt for a time to give yourself lower payments, you can go one of two ways. You can contact the lenders yourself, and try to work something out. Lenders typically advise this, and if you've just been laid off, or have had some mishap occur and think you can remedy the situation with time, you might want to handle negotiations yourself. You can also try writing to credit bureaus to get a brief statement included in your credit report outlining how you've corrected your debt problems.

Don't hook up with so called "credit repair" outfits that advertise that they can fix your credit record for a fee. They can't do anything you can't do by yourself, or with the help of legitimate consumer groups. One legitimate organization is the National Center for Financial Education, a non-profit consumer group that publishes or distributes lots of good nuts-and-bolts financial and credit information. The NCFE is based in California, at P.O. Box 34070, San Diego, CA 92163. Include a stamped, self-addressed envelope if you want them to send you information on the many kinds of brochures they offer. Another group is the Bankcard Holders of America, an association of credit card consumers, headquartered in Virginia and known for tracking the cheapest cards (phone 540-389-5445). BHA has also developed a system consumers can customize to figure out how best to eradicate debt, called Debt Zapper. It is available for $15 by writing to BHA Debt Zapper, 524 Branch Drive, Salem, VA 24153. The Debt Zapper works by taking a little more than you're already paying now, and prioritizing your debts according to the interest rate you're paying. After you get one creditor paid off, you can apply that money to the next creditor in line, and the increases you're using will wipe out your debt much faster than if you just continued to make minimum payments to each creditor.

If the situation is already out of hand, and you can't negotiate with creditors, or feel too overwhelmed or depressed to try, contact Consumer Credit Counseling Services (CCCS) at 1-800-388-2227, or look on the World Wide Web at the home page for The National Foundation for Consumer Credit Counseling at http://www.nfcc.org. CCCS can go over your budget with you, and set up a debt repayment plan in which your local office works with the creditors on your behalf. In that way, you get some objective advice and an ally with some clout with creditors. You'll have to repay your bills and it may take time, but you'll have a buffer between you and collection agencies while you're trying to remedy your income and credit situation.

Your last, last, last resort should be bankruptcy, the court filing that reorders your financial life. Often in the case of bankruptcy, a couple of factors have combined to push someone over the edge, such as a job loss, an illness, a divorce, or an accident. You can see that these things can happen unexpectedly, and be difficult shocks in themselves to absorb.

BANKCARD HOLDERS OF AMERICA
524 BRANCH DRIVE
SALEM, VIRGINIA 24153, 703/389-5445

A non-profit organization helping bankcard holders become informed consumers.

DEBT ZAPPER SAMPLE SAVINGS SUMMARY

Financial Profile <u>Without</u> BHA's DEBT ZAPPER:		Financial Profile <u>Using</u> ($10 more per month) BHA's DEBT ZAPPER:	
Total Debts:	$1,900	Total Debts:	$1,900
Interest Paid:	$4,097	Interest Paid:	$1,019
Total Money Paid:	$5,997	Total Money Paid:	$2,919
Number of Years:	23 yrs 3 mos	Number of Years:	5 yrs 2 mos

TOTAL SAVINGS USING BHA'S DEBT ZAPPER:

TIME SAVED:	217 MONTHS (18 years)
MONEY SAVED:	$3,078

---

* This assumes an 18% APR and a 2% ($15) minimum payment.

BANKCARD HOLDERS OF AMERICA
524 BRANCH DRIVE
SALEM, VIRGINIA 24153, 703/389-5445

A non-profit organization helping bankcard holders become informed consumers.

THIS DEBT ZAPPER REPORT WAS
SPECIALLY PREPARED FOR:
EXAMPLE
MR & MRS CONSUMER
1234 MAIN ST
ANYTOWN USA 12345

USING BHA'S DEBT ZAPPER,
YOU'LL SAVE $7,362.93
AND 245 MONTHS OF PAYMENTS.

THIS IS THE DEBT ZAPPER
YOU REQUESTED FROM
BANKCARD HOLDERS OF AMERICA

This report was specially prepared for you, at your request, by the staff of BankCard Holders of America.

For each of your credit cards listed, you can pay off your outstanding balance in the shortest possible time -- at the lowest possible cost -- by paying the monthly amounts indicated on each card.

This analysis is based on your application information, including the amount you currently owe on each card, the interest rate on each card, the minimum payment required by each card issuer, and the total amount you are prepared to pay toward your credit card bills each month.

This report includes three (3) important sections:

• Section I details exactly how much you should pay each month -- on each of your credit cards -- until they are all completely paid off;

• Section II details what your remaining outstanding debt will be -- each month on each card -- if you follow the payoff schedule outlined in Section I;

• Section III summarizes the savings you'll enjoy, in the time required to pay off your credit card debts and the actual dollars you'll save in finance charges, by using DEBT ZAPPER.

You've made a wise decision to slash your credit card debt with DEBT ZAPPER. Just think how good you'll feel when all your credit card debts are paid off -- and now that day is a lot closer than ever before!

SECTION I

MONTHLY PAYMENT SCHEDULE

Total Monthly Payment $210*

Each month, just pay the exact amounts we recommend on the credit cards listed below and you'll pay off your debts in the most efficient way possible.

Monthly Payments For 1996

Creditor	Jan	Feb	Mar	Apr	May	Jun	Jul	Aug	Sep	Oct	Nov	Dec
SPEIGEL	***	***	***	***	***	***	***	***	***	$25	43	49
SEARS	***	***	***	***	***	***	***	***	***	$19	19	19
DISCOVER	***	***	***	***	***	***	***	***	***	$23	23	23
VISA	***	***	***	***	***	***	***	***	***	$39	39	39
JC PENNEY	***	***	***	***	***	***	***	***	***	$48	41	35
MASTERCARD	***	***	***	***	***	***	***	***	***	$46	45	45

Monthly Payments For 1997

Creditor	Jan	Feb	Mar	Apr	May	Jun	Jul	Aug	Sep	Oct	Nov	Dec
SPEIGEL	$55	59	66	26	***	***	***	***	***	***	***	***
SEARS	$19	19	18	61	87	88	88	90	90	108	111	111
DISCOVER	$23	23	23	22	22	22	22	22	22	22	22	22
VISA	$39	39	38	38	38	38	38	37	37	37	37	37
JC PENNEY	$30	26	22	20	20	20	20	20	20	3	***	***
MASTERCARD	$44	44	43	43	43	42	42	41	41	40	40	40

Monthly Payments For 1998

Creditor	Jan	Feb	Mar	Apr	May	Jun	Jul	Aug	Sep	Oct	Nov	Dec
SEARS	$9	***	***	***	***	***	***	***	***	***	***	***
DISCOVER	$133	135	136	136	136	137	138	138	17	***	***	***
VISA	$36	36	36	36	36	36	35	35	157	174	175	175
MASTERCARD	$39	39	38	38	38	37	37	37	36	36	35	35

Monthly Payments For 1999

Creditor	Jan	Feb	Mar	Apr	May	Jun	Jul	Aug	Sep	Oct	Nov	Dec
VISA	$175	176	176	176	177	177	175	***	***	***	***	***
MASTERCARD	$35	34	34	34	33	33	36	210	210	210	210	210

*Note: This report reflects the extra $10 a month you have indicated you are willing and able to pay to retire your debts more quickly and at much less expense, assuming you make <u>no new</u> charges. We've started your payoff schedule in the <u>upcoming</u> month, so you can start fresh with your next set of credit card bills.

DEBT ZAPPER is a service provided for credit card consumers by Bankcard Holders of America, a national non-profit consumer protection and advocacy organization.

SECTION I

MONTHLY PAYMENT SCHEDULE

Total Monthly Payment $210*

Each month, just pay the exact amounts we recommend on the credit cards listed below and you'll pay off your debts in the most efficient way possible.

Creditor	Jan	Feb	Monthly Payments For 2000 Mar	Apr	May	Jun	Jul	Aug	Sep	Oct	Nov	Dec
MASTERCARD	$210	99	***	***	***	***	***	***	***	***	***	***

*Note: This report reflects the extra $10 a month you have indicated you are willing and able to pay to retire your debts more quickly and at much less expense, assuming you make no new charges. We've started your payoff schedule in the upcoming month, so you can start fresh with your next set of credit card bills.

DEBT ZAPPER is a service provided for credit card consumers by Bankcard Holders of America, a national non-profit consumer protection and advocacy organization.

SECTION II

MONTHLY BALANCE REPORT

Total Monthly Payment $210

This chart details what your actual outstanding monthly <u>balances</u> will be on each of your credit cards if you pay the amounts recommended in Section I (the <u>MONTHLY PAYMENT SCHEDULE</u>).

(<u>Note:</u> These are <u>not</u> the amounts you have to pay each month!)

Monthly Balances For 1996

Creditor	Jan	Feb	Mar	Apr	May	Jun	Jul	Aug	Sep	Oct	Nov	Dec
SPEIGEL	***	***	***	***	***	***	***	***	***	$281	243	198
SEARS	***	***	***	***	***	***	***	***	***	$795	790	785
DISCOVER	***	***	***	***	***	***	***	***	***	$1095	1090	1085
VISA	***	***	***	***	***	***	***	***	***	$1956	1947	1937
JC PENNEY	***	***	***	***	***	***	***	***	***	$256	219	188
MASTERCARD	***	***	***	***	***	***	***	***	***	$1812	1794	1775

Monthly Balances For 1997

Creditor	Jan	Feb	Mar	Apr	May	Jun	Jul	Aug	Sep	Oct	Nov	Dec
SPEIGEL	$147	90	26	***	***	***	***	***	***	***	***	***
SEARS	$779	774	770	722	647	570	492	411	327	225	118	9
DISCOVER	$1080	1075	1070	1065	1061	1056	1052	1047	1042	1038	1033	1028
VISA	$1927	1917	1907	1898	1888	1879	1869	1860	1851	1842	1832	1823
JC PENNEY	$160	137	117	99	80	61	42	23	3	***	***	***
MASTERCARD	$1758	1740	1722	1705	1687	1670	1652	1636	1619	1603	1586	1570

Monthly Balances For 1998

Creditor	Jan	Feb	Mar	Apr	May	Jun	Jul	Aug	Sep	Oct	Nov	Dec
DISCOVER	$912	792	669	544	416	286	152	17	***	***	***	***
VISA	$1814	1805	1796	1787	1778	1769	1760	1752	1621	1471	1318	1162
MASTERCARD	$1554	1538	1522	1507	1491	1476	1461	1445	1431	1416	1402	1387

Monthly Balances For 1999

Creditor	Jan	Feb	Mar	Apr	May	Jun	Jul	Aug	Sep	Oct	Nov	Dec
VISA	$1005	843	680	514	344	172	***	***	***	***	***	***
MASTERCARD	$1373	1359	1345	1331	1318	1304	1288	1097	902	706	506	303

SECTION II

MONTHLY BALANCE REPORT

Total Monthly Payment $210

This chart details what your actual outstanding monthly <u>balances</u> will be on each of your credit cards if you pay the amounts recommended in Section I (the <u>MONTHLY PAYMENT SCHEDULE</u>).

(<u>Note:</u> These are <u>not</u> the amounts you have to pay each month!)

Creditor	Jan	Feb	Mar	Apr	May	Jun	Jul	Aug	Sep	Oct	Nov	Dec
				Monthly Balances For 2000								
MASTERCARD	$97	***	***	***	***	***	***	***	***	***	***	***

SECTION III

DEBT ZAPPER SAVINGS SUMMARY

Payoff Priority		Creditor	APR	Starting Balance	Pmt %
Priority	1	SPEIGEL	22.60%	$ 300.00	3.00%
Priority	2	SEARS	21.00%	800.00	2.38%
Priority	3	DISCOVER	19.80%	1,100.00	2.10%
Priority	4	VISA	18.00%	1,966.00	2.00%
Priority	5	JC PENNEY	18.00%	300.00	16.00%
Priority	6	MASTERCARD	17.70%	1,831.00	2.50%

Financial Profile Without BHA's DEBT ZAPPER		VS.	Financial Profile Using BHA's DEBT ZAPPER	
Your total debts	$6,297.00	VS.	Your total debts	$6,297.00
Interest you'll pay	$9,570.08	VS.	Interest you'll pay	$2,207.15
Total money you'll pay	$15,867.08	VS.	Total money you'll pay	$8,504.15
Number of months required	286	VS.	Number of months required	41

TOTAL SAVINGS USING BHA'S DEBT ZAPPER:

TIME SAVED: 245 MONTHS
MONEY SAVED: $7,362.93

DEBT ZAPPER is a service provided for credit card consumers by Bankcard Holders of America, a national non-profit consumer protection and advocacy organization.

Rebuilding Your Credit with a Secured Card

If you've had all your credit cards yanked, which can happen if you get deep enough into debt, but you've been able to rectify the situation and pay back the debts, you'll probably want to get started on rebuilding credit. Not that you'll want to repeat any past spending patterns that got you into trouble before, but because you'll probably still need a credit history for home or auto loans, or maybe a card for identification or travel purposes.

Bankcard Holders of America says that using a secured card for a year or two and making timely payments that get reported to the credit bureaus will help you rebuild a credit history. BHA makes a list of legitimate secured card holders that you can get by sending $4 to its address at 524 Branch Drive, Salem, VA 24153. The group says you need to consider these factors when you're shopping for a secured card:

- How much of a deposit the card company wants, because this money will be tied up and unavailable for you to use.

- How much credit you get for your deposit—it can be as little as 50 percent of your deposit, or as much as 50 percent more of your deposit.

- How much interest you'll earn on your deposit.

- How much you will be charged for an annual fee and application fee.

- Be sure the issuer doesn't require you to make the deposit until they've already approved the card.

- Make sure the issuer will report your payment history to credit bureaus, but also make sure they don't report the card as a secured card, but only as a credit card.

Action Items

Establish a realistic attitude about credit card use as an instrument of debt and not a means to increase income, or a way of financing a lifestyle beyond your earnings.

....

Watch financially responsible people in your line of work or with similar earnings and gear your lifestyle expectations accordingly. Don't expect to immediately replicate the same lifestyle your parents achieved after years of work.

....

Note your debt-to-income ratios when working with your spending plan or budget. You can make decreasing that ratio one of your goals.

....

Action Items

(Continued)

Close out charge accounts that you aren't using or don't need. Try to pare back the cards to one or two, or in rare instances, three.

....

Consider buying items on layaway. Many discount stores offer layaway, but ask small shops about this option if you don't see signs posted.

....

Keep abreast of newspaper, magazine, and newsletter articles about developments in the credit card industry. That way you'll know about new things the card issuers are always doing to pump up profits, and get a constant supply of tips on cutting credit costs. Two good sources of information on this subject are Robert Heady's weekly column, syndicated in many newspapers, and a quarterly newsletter called The Pocket Change Investor (1-800-255-0899), published quarterly for $12.95 a year.

....

If your cash flow is good, but you keep running up debt, consider whether something nonfinancial is the crux of the problem, and seek appropriate counseling. One place to look is the Debtors' Anonymous listing in your phone book.

CASE IN POINT:

Plastic Pitfalls

Kathryn Bickford, a certified financial planner in Stratham, New Hampshire, recalls a young woman whose credit card habits were getting in the way of her other goals.

The young woman was smart, conscientious, wanted to help others, but was rather aimless financially. She was sharing an apartment with two roommates and was making $27,000 as an administrative assistant. She felt that her college career was being followed by a cycle of debts, working, and more debts.

And she had a lot of debts $25,174 in student loans, and another $11,000 in credit cards. Her monthly rent and utilities cost was $468, she drove an old car, and didn't have any savings. Bickford found out the woman was spending too much on vacations and entertainment—more than 10 percent of her income. That was more than the woman could afford, Bickford said. Her advice: cut the entertainment budget by half by finding less expensive vacations and diversions. That alone, Bickford said, would give this woman an extra $1,100 to $1,200 a year she could use to pay down her credit card debt. The goal would be to pay off the higher-debt credit cards first, then the lower debt ones. Cutting back this way would also give the college graduate another $100 a month she could use to work down her student loan debts.

Meanwhile, to keep from falling back into the credit card habit, the woman would need to get some savings going. Then if she ran into a problem with her old car, for example, the repairs wouldn't have to be put on her credit card.

Chapter 7

Shopping Strategies

To all sorts of manufacturers,
retailers, and entertainment companies, you're a darling demographic. Your earnings
potential, your sophistication, your sex appeal, your needs for clothing, eyewear, housing, furniture, intellectual and cultural stimulation, computer software and hardware,
transportation, travel, and more, make you the kind of customer companies want. From
apparel to books and from movies to cars, they've got something to sell you. And they
have lots of ways to sell these items to hip, technologically sophisticated consumers
like you. They'll get it to you through catalogs, discount stores, department stores, specialty boutiques, over the Internet—whatever it takes. Marketers are always dreaming
up new promotions or distribution vehicles or recycling old ones. For all their glitz and
gimmicks, though, you have the power. You decide whether to spend and how much.

It's smart to know a little bit about how stores operate, and when and how you can
manage to make the best purchases. Best doesn't always mean the least expensive, of
course. Depending on the nature of the item, you'll want to consider value, which is

determined by factors such as ease of use, durability, and more. The computer you can get most inexpensively may not have the power and graphics you could use, or may not be most compatible with the systems you have at work. The raincoat that's the least costly might not be as well constructed, rain resistant, or durable as one that costs $20 more. Frequently, the value an item brings you will affect how well you feel about the purchase later. Sometimes you regret spending the money; sometimes you think it was money put to good use.

Stores and Their Design

Supermarkets and other kinds of stores are known for using floor plans that encourage consumers to buy the most. It's a long walk in many markets—past seasonal items like summer yard furniture, impulse buys such as candy, and video racks—just to get to the milk and the bread. Similarly, in clothing stores and discount outlets, the basic underwear, jeans, skirts, and tops are often found beyond more trendy and perhaps profitable items in front, such as decorative sweaters or more expensive outerwear.

Cross merchandising is another way of capturing shoppers' attention. This is a practice of displaying a couple of different items together so that when you see the first item you were intending to buy anyway, you also consider buying a secondary item. For example, in the summer you might find some of the stock of strawberry shortcake shells or whipped cream moved out of the bread and dairy aisle into the fresh produce area with the berries. Then you'll start thinking about buying the extra ingredients to make strawberry shortcake, whereas before you only had been thinking generally about buying some fruit, or perhaps just buying strawberries to put on your breakfast cereal.

For the person with limited income and time, the best defense against being sucked into overspending is to be armed with a shopping list. You don't need to be militant about it, but inventory what you need before you leave the house, and shop according to the list. If you see some sale items that you will eventually need, like batteries or light bulbs, and have the cash on hand to afford it, then it makes financial sense to buy something not on the list.

Tips on Buying Food

You really can make a difference in your food budget by buying wisely and limiting the amount of times you eat out. Here are some strategies for handling the food budget:

- Use unit pricing in the supermarket, which allows you to compare the costs of items per increment of measure. It really works, and you'll often find that buying larger quantities saves money. You may not have the space to store a huge box of breakfast cereal, but you may be able to buy the medium-sized container of mayonnaise and find that it saves you money over the smaller jar.

- Buy store brands. They're cheaper.

- Use coupons for things you would normally buy. Coupons have gotten harder to use in recent years, with shorter expiration periods and discounts sometimes limited to multiple purchases. Often you find coupons only on more expensive items that you might normally bypass. Consequently, some people don't bother with coupons anymore. It's a waste of time to clip and organize coupons you won't use, but if you're efficient about it and concentrate your efforts only on key items, you can still save money using them.

- Consider bulk purchases of nonperishables with a buying buddy, like a housemate, a neighbor, or a friend from work. This way you might be able to share purchases of items available in bigger quantities or at warehouse clubs.

- In season, shop at a farmer's market. They might not deliver cheaper prices, but the produce is quite fresh and because of that, may last longer than what you can get at a supermarket.

- Shop for your basic nutritional and health requirements first, for entertainment or luxury items second. Protein, carbohydrates, and even vitamins should take precedence on your shopping list.

Tips on Buying Clothing

Outfitting yourself in your first work wardrobe can be an expensive undertaking. This makes clothing money a great graduation present.

There are a few things you need to keep in mind about your work and nonwork clothing expenditures. There's an old saying that if you want to move up in a company or field, you should dress like the people at the level where you want to be. Having the right look sure doesn't hurt. But there's a certain amount of room for negotiation in applying this. Not every impressive supervisor is spending the most possible on clothes, you'll notice. You need a wardrobe that's appropriate, not necessarily trendy or extremely expensive. If you use the fashion catalogs or layouts of young men's and women's magazines as your guide, however, you can spend hundreds on blazers, shoes, shirts, and accessories. Separate fashion hype from your necessities. Overspending on clothes won't make you a career success.

- Take an inventory of your clothing needs before shopping, and keep in mind what basic colors and items you need or already have that can be coordinated with new purchases. This will give you the most versatile, functional wardrobe possible. Tell your family what colors they should look for if they buy you clothing for gifts, adds Pam Norum, associate professor of textile and apparel management at the University of Missouri at Columbia.

- If you have the time, try buying clothing at the end of the season, or during preseason sales when stores want to clear out inventory and offer the best prices. This works with items like winter coats, boots, and other seasonal apparel. On the other hand, if you need boots before a blizzard, you need them. The other potential pitfall with this method is that you may not find what you need in your size by the time the clearance sale rolls around.

- When store or catalog shopping, ask the staff if any sales are coming up.

- When you decide to buy something from a catalog, rip out the page, order form, and your mailing address information and recycle the rest. That way you won't be tempted by extraneous items on other pages of the catalog.

- Don't overlook well-run consignment stores with good merchandise. They can save you a bundle. If and when you have small children, consignment shops are particularly good for their clothing needs, since smaller children outgrow clothing before it can be worn out. For women, new maternity wear is also expensive. Tag sales are another option, but shopping this way can be a time-consuming, hit-or-miss proposition. Don't count on it. Be pleasantly surprised and grateful when it works out.

- Stay away from clothing that requires dry cleaning, which costs more, or hand washing, which may take extra time at home or at the Laundromat.

- In urban areas, off-price outlets can be the best option. Factory outlets can be good options too, but some sell designer clothing so expensive that even marked down it's out of your price range. Discount stores can be good for basic clothing stock, like turtlenecks, underwear, and socks, though they may be more limited in their supply of clothing you can wear to an office. Also, buy trendier items and fashion accessories at discount stores when you want to update your clothing, Norum advises.

- Some young people especially like to organize clothing exchanges where they can trade outfits with each other that they don't want anymore, Norum notes, "It can be almost like a party."

- If you have to wear a uniform to work that you really couldn't wear elsewhere, keep the receipts because you may be able to deduct from your federal income taxes the costs of purchasing and caring for the clothing. The tax code is pretty specific about this kind of deduction, though. The Internal Revenue Service means for this deduction to be used by people who have to wear special safety shoes in a factory, airline pilots, hospital workers, letter carriers, and so on. It's not for people who buy nicer suits to impress clients or bosses.

Furniture, Appliances, and Electronics

Keep in mind that you don't really need to acquire every piece of electronics on the showroom floor at once. But when you first move into an apartment or house, you'd be surprised at how much money you can spend on curtain rods, a food processor, wastebaskets, linens, and a few household tools. In many instances, you can get used items to start with. People get rid of things long before they wear out because they're moving, redecorating, or moving up to a new model.

- Cruise garage sales and tag sales for household items in particular. You'll find useful items at a fraction of the retail cost. Newspaper ads in smaller cities may be another consideration, but you may have safety concerns about visiting the homes of strangers.

- Watch for sales, discontinued merchandise, and floor models.

- Beware of so-called "zero financing" promotions to sell new merchandise. Typically, the ads will say that you won't pay any interest or payments for six months, and you have the option of paying off the full amount. But often, if you haven't paid off the sum, the "zero interest" that was suspended for six months is suddenly charged retroactively. You then are paying higher store credit charges than if you had bought the appliance or item of furniture with a major credit card.

- Take advantage of layaway.

- Stay away from "rent-to-own" options unless you're on a short-term job assignment, like three to six months, in a place away from your normal home. The charges over time for this furniture are much higher than its usual retail cost. If you're in a pinch, you're much better off buying used.

- Secondhand shops can be useful, but you might find "secondhand antique shops" too expensive.

- If you need to get a home computer for work, see if your employer will cover any of the cost. New computers keep coming down in price and it may not be worth it to buy a used model unless it's a second system, like a laptop just for added convenience.

Bartering

What if you could trade resume-creating services for an oil change or some other valued service without laying out the cash? As long as you trusted the other party, and found the timing convenient, you'd probably think that was a good deal. Bartering seems to be coming into vogue again. It's always been done informally between friends on a one-to-one basis. In some areas of the country, there are bartering networks that can put you in touch with people you haven't met before. You might provide your service to the general network, and be able to receive a service in exchange. Sometimes this works particularly well for small businesses that, like individuals, can have a limited cash flow. If you're interested in this, ask your area chamber of commerce about any bartering arrangements that may be operating in your area. Be aware of the fact that bartering income and sales can be considered taxable, just like routine exchanges of currency.

Smaller, Day-to-Day Items

Keep the following tips in mind when making routine, recurring purchases:

- Try to go for generic and name-brand medicines when you need them. Ask your doctor about how much prescriptions cost and if there are suitable, less expensive options on the market for your needs. Apply the same strategy when buying contact lenses and solutions.

- Comparison shop on personal care services like hair styling.

- Always look for the most inexpensive options in parking and transportation, while keeping yourself safe.

Holidays and Birthday Gifts and Such

There are a couple of different schools of thought on gift giving. One holds that you should buy items the person needs. Another holds that you should buy fun items the person wouldn't necessarily buy for themselves. A middle-of-the-road strategy is to try to combine both elements, perhaps in a two-part gift. Notice in none of these scenarios does anyone suggest you need to buy the most expensive gift possible.

For family and friends, gift giving seems to work best when you can keep the preferences and needs of the receiver in mind well in advance of the event. That way, when you see something they would like, might need, or the item is on sale, you can get it then and put it away. This assumes that you listen to family and friends carefully, and pay attention to their routines, of course. Waiting until the last minute and then just guessing at what they want is likely to cost more money and produce a gift that isn't as special.

If your funds are limited, one way to keep your costs down is to go in on a gift with someone else and share the costs. This works with siblings, for example, and also for gifts for coworkers. Showers and going away celebrations have a way of developing in workplaces whether or not you planned for them in your budget. These instances can be a pain, but the reality is that often you'll want to participate, just for smooth working relations. If you can't share the cost of a gift with someone, buy something that you can afford, maybe a half pound of gourmet coffee or a small plant. You can always make something or volunteer a service, but make sure it's appropriate to the circumstance. Babysitting for your sister-in-law is one thing; watching one of your coworker's little ones may be more goodwill than you want to spend.

Weddings and Other Big Celebrations

Somehow shopping for unusual family events can mushroom into huge budget items. People who normally budget well for food and clothing can find themselves caught up in thousands of dollars worth of regalia if they are planning a wedding or commitment ceremony. Weddings nationally have an average cost of $15,000 in recent years. The amount varies somewhat by region of the country, but even given that, if you go by the averages, the expense of a traditional wedding outstrips the average undergraduate student loan debt. And people complain about college loans! The biggest expense in the wedding is usually the reception. You can cut costs by limiting the guest list, looking at less expensive meals (simple receptions with just punch or cake), or booking a hall at off-peak days, hours, or times of the year. And if you're willing to wear clothes not normally sold as wedding attire, but are nonetheless beautiful, you can save money there too. Weddings should be looked at as mega-shopping decisions where there is always a simpler, less expensive alternative. The bridal industry offers many checklists, guides, and magazines giving detailed advice about planning and economizing on weddings. Use them, and consider the importance of the actual expense to those involved, before committing to a financial encumbrance that could set you back for years.

Action Items

Use your normal shopping expeditions as opportunities to practice bargain hunting, planning, and goal setting. You'll get consistently better at it.

Try to sleep on a major purchase before committing yourself. A little bit of time can give you perspective on how much you're willing to spend. Comparison shop and research items in publications such as Consumer Reports and Consumer Guide.

Read consumer magazines from time to time to get a sense of the best deals on everything from soap to computers.

Action Items

(Continued)

Consider asking for gift certificates for gifts—even supermarkets make them available now.

....

Try shopping with a significant other a number of times if you're considering merging households. This will give you some information about how compatible your money styles are and what differences may need sorting out.

Chapter 8

Negotiating

Back when you were a small child
and you stood in the aisle of a store and pleaded with a parent for the purchase of a cereal, a toy, or a game, you were negotiating. You may have been promising you'd be good. You may have been articulating that the item was needed, it was the thing to have. Your simple persistence may have been the biggest bargaining chip you held in these dealing with grown-ups.

Somehow, many people seem to lose the boldness and creativity needed to negotiate as they come into adulthood. Whining as you did when you were a child is certainly no longer appropriate, but other strategies are. Why don't you use them? Maybe you just don't know what they are. Sometimes you may not recognize when there's an opportunity to negotiate and think of negotiating as being applicable only to international peace relations, boundary disputes, and maybe car buying. Yet, there are plenty of opportunities to negotiate when taking a job, making a purchase, or working out chores or divisions of financial responsibility with a housemate. If you don't practice your negotiating skills, you're apt to miss chances to improve situations for yourself.

Or you may feel vaguely resentful and shortchanged after certain encounters, without really being able to pinpoint how things may have turned out more to your liking.

What Negotiating Entails

Steven P. Cohen, a Massachusetts negotiator and mediator who runs a training firm called The Negotiation Skills Company, likes to say that negotiating helps people reach decisions jointly "in a civilized way." (The company offers advice on its Web site at http://www.negotiationskills.com.) That depiction makes sense: If people didn't negotiate, the options would be one person intimidating or dictating conditions, or perhaps one party abdicating interest in any given situation.

Cohen says that negotiating requires multiple steps. First, you have to know what you really want, why and how badly you want or need it, and at what point you're willing to walk away without getting it. Second, you've got to know what the other party wants and why it's important to them. This is vital information if you're going to craft some creative resolution that will satisfy everyone. Also, how much do they need or want what you have to offer? What would make them really happy? Does their behavior demonstrate honesty and sincerity, indicating you can trust them to follow through on their word? Some people are going to be upfront with you when you ask what they want, others are going to be more guarded and perhaps afraid that you've got some secret agenda to trick them.

How much time you spend on this kind of discussion and bargaining research depends on what you want and the nature of your relationship with the person. You may be able to observe a lot about your boss—how much she values punctuality and order and quiet, for example. It may not be worth your time to ask lots of questions about every assignment your boss hands down. You can tell what your boss wants from observation.

On the other hand, if you keep getting more and more projects loaded onto you at work, it may be worth several conversations with your boss to negotiate your working conditions, and his or her satisfaction with your job performance. Using Cohen's approach, you might ask your boss questions like:

- How important is this project compared to the one I'm already working on in terms of my time commitment? How about the deadline?

- Is there anything you want me to do differently with these projects than the previous ones we've handled?

- How do the higher-ups view this project or client?

- Is there any data or any resources already available that would help me finish this faster for you?

- Should I work under an overtime pay schedule to get this done for you? Alternatively, depending on your work situation, you might try: If I work late to get this done quickly, will I be able to take some comp time next week or at some other time?

If you can approach this situation in a helpful, interested way, without seeming challenging or complaining, in most instances you're likely to get the best result: clear objectives from your boss, perhaps some help on the project, and compensation for added time on the job. If the opposite is true, and the your boss is uncommunicative, defiant, or unhelpful, you've got to know for your own well-being when it's best to walk away. Some people aren't good business partners, reasonable suppliers, or fair employers. You might not discover that in a single attempt at negotiation, but over time such patterns will become apparent. You then have to decide if that's a good place for you to be. If you're negotiating a one-shot deal, such as the purchase of a stereo system, you've still got to know when you can't reach amiable, agreeable terms, and when it would be better for you to pass on a given deal and either shop for another opportunity, or wait for one to emerge.

Some Possible Subjects of Financial Negotiations

The topics that can be negotiated are wide-ranging. Here are just a few that have financial ramifications:

- More money, better working conditions, less work, or more vacation, for yourself or for your bargaining unit if you're unionized

- A car lease or purchase

- An agreement about who pays certain bills at home

- An agreement to switch shifts with a coworker

- A creditor's willingness to let you delay a payment because you've just gotten laid off

- A discount on the rent in return for mowing the lawn

- New paint paid for by the landlord in return for your labor in repainting the living room

- A sabbatical when the terms aren't clearly spelled out in the employee handbook

- A discount because a piece of merchandise you want, a book or an item of clothing, for example, has a small stain or tear

- A divorce

- A credit card with the annual fee waived

- Free delivery on a big appliance you've purchased

- A repair contract for your condo's roof, on behalf of your condo association

- A graduate-school fellowship

When you look at negotiations in this light, you can see how often the skill can be useful in everyday life. You can also see that in negotiations for big-ticket items like cars, apartment rents, and so on, there's not much room for acting only on impulse. You really have to think about what purchase or agreement would make the most sense for you. And to know that, you almost certainly have to comparison shop to understand prices and supplies.

How to Practice Your Negotiating Skills

Start out with low-intensity, congenial settings where you can talk and chat and where the stakes aren't very high. A farmer's market or a yard sale can be such a setting. If the prices aren't marked, you're almost led into negotiations, because you have to ask the seller how much he or she wants for an item. Late in the day of the sale, the seller may be willing to settle for less than before or he or she may accept an entirely different price for buying two or three items in bulk.

In relationships, families, and work settings, you may want to start small on your negotiating skills if you've rarely asserted yourself in the past. When you start asking for what you want, the other parties will sense the rules of the game are shifting and react with surprise or dismay. That, in turn, can shake your confidence, and you might back down before you realize what has happened. So it's easier for some people to start out in matters of smaller consequences, where possible, and build confidence and self-assurance.

In some sales situations, or other settings where someone is trying to convince you of something, the other party will make it easy for you to practice negotiating. They'll just come out and ask: What can I do to convince you or to earn your business? And you'll be able to tell them what you want, whether you feel you can even consider the deal or position they're offering, or if you'd rather not participate in the situation.

Action Items

Think about past encounters where you weren't satisfied with what you got. Imagine how the dialogue would have been different, and what you would have said to have achieved the goal you really wanted.

....

Make a practice of observing how people who are good negotiators operate, whether it's a sibling or a boss talking to a peer. You may not always get a chance to be a fly on the wall, so ask people you can trust what suggestions and counter-suggestions were useful in coming to agreements they've made. For example, you can ask: How did it go with accounting? What did the vendor offer?

....

Keep your emotions—fear, anger, desire, and so on—in balance so that they don't overpower your best judgment.

Chapter 9

Transportation

If you don't have a car, and live

in a city where there's reliable public transportation, count yourself lucky. Your options won't be complicated by parking, auto repair, insurance, and other encumbrances that come with having a car. You can try to cut any public transportation fees by looking into monthly passes that may be offered by your transportation authority, and when it's safe, by walking or riding a bike.

After you have a car, life gets more complicated. In working life, cars don't have the same feelings of freedom and flexibility they seem to deliver to many people during adolescence. The car becomes your means of getting to work, while it also demands that you work to pay for the gasoline and upkeep. Transportation can be one of your biggest expenses. The stark truth, according to the American Automobile Association (AAA), is that the person who drove a conservative 15,000 miles in 1996 had to come up with $6,465 to do so. AAA figures that in July, August, and September of 1996, for example, motorists spent 43.1 cents a mile to keep their cars going. That figure takes into account gasoline, oil, tires, maintenance, insurance, registration, taxes, and financing. Some areas of the country cost a little more, and some less, as this chart shows.

One of the ways to keep transportation costs under control is to look at cars as strictly utilitarian, meaning you buy them for your transportation needs, not for your image. You want good gas mileage more than a plush interior. You need a reliable car that requires relatively little maintenance as opposed to a flashy car. You want something that costs a reasonable amount to insure, not something that increases your cost of operation. Young drivers, particularly young male drivers, already face higher auto insurance costs because of the number of accidents they, as a population, are prone to. Whether you buy new or used, or lease, keep in mind that utility is more important than flash.

Leasing may be a good option for people in sales fields who need a late-model, reliable car. The thing you have to remember with the lease, though, is it is just rent. At the end of a lease period, you don't own the car and you might have spent as much financing a car you would own outright at the end of the financing period. And new cars these days last longer, to 100,000 miles or more, so if your car is for basic transportation, it may make more sense to buy one, even though the value starts to decline (depreciate) as soon as you buy it.

Here are some of the approximate prices for economy-type new 1997 automobiles, as reported in the fall season when the cars are first shown for the model year:

Ford Aspire	$9,000
Dodge/Plymouth Neon	$10,400
Geo Metro	$8,500
Saturn SL/SL1/SL2	$10,500
Hyundai Accent	$8,600
Honda Civic	$10,500
Mitsubishi Mirage	$10,400
Suzuki Swift	$9,500
Toyota Tercel	$10,800

Before deciding on a vehicle, of course you need to check the reliability ratings in consumer magazines like *Consumer Reports*. If you're buying used, the reliability ratings will be even more important to you, and you'll want to have the vehicle inspected by a mechanic before you buy. Check used prices offered you against a price guide called *Kelley's Blue Book*. More options are opening up these days to buy used. There are used cars that come off of leasing programs and then are sold, and also chains of used-car sales outlets are trying to give the industry a more professional image.

COSTS OF OPERATING A CAR: JULY–SEPTEMBER 1996

(Based on driving 15,000 miles a year)

National average	43.1 cents a mile or $6,465 a year
New England	45 cents a mile or $6,750 a year
Mid-Atlantic	43.8 cents a mile or $6,570 a year
Great Lakes	42.3 cents a mile or $6,345 a year
Midwest	41.9 cents a mile or $6,285 a year
Southeast	42 cents a mile or $6,300 a year
West	43.9 cents a mile or $6,585 a year
Southwest	43.5 cents a mile or $6,525 a year

Source: American Automobile Association, based on a composite average of a subcompact Ford Escort LX, a mid-size Ford Taurus GL, and a full-size Chevrolet Caprice Classic

Financing a Car

Some people save enough money to buy their vehicles outright for cash (more on that later). Typically, though, when you buy a car, you've got to come up with a way to pay for the car over time because you can't afford the thousands of dollars it will probably cost in one bite.

If you get financing either from a car dealer, a credit union, or a bank, you'll be expected to come up with some kind of down payment, and then arrive at a plan for paying off the balance over time, through monthly payments.

In the past few years, it's become more common for lenders to offer longer terms on auto loans; for example, to let a borrower pay off a car over five years instead of three or four years. This may make the monthly payment smaller, but it may not be such a great idea. A lot of things can happen in five years, after all. Your car can get totaled, for one thing, and you may have to replace it. If the insurance money for the current value of the car doesn't cover the debt still owed, you'll be "upside down." Then you'll need a new car and you'll be paying for two cars at once, even though you're only driving one. Author and financial expert Jonathan Pond has a rule of thumb that's helpful in these matters: Don't finance a car for more than three years. If you can't swing the payments in that period, you can't afford that particular car, and will have to look at another one.

With that advice in mind, you can proceed to think about other things you're going to need to compare in buying a car. First, find out from insurance companies how much it costs to insure the kind of cars you're looking at: Some vehicles are bigger theft or accident risks, and therefore cost more to insure. Who can give you the best interest rate? Realize the interest rates on used vehicles are higher, because financing a used car is a bigger risk for a lender than financing a new car. Can you get any deals if you're buying your first new car? If the dealers are pushing rebates on a particular car, is it because the car is a slow seller, and one that you might not particularly want? On the other hand, if the car you want is out of reach, have you made sure you've got a couple of other options in mind that would suit your purposes? It's ill-advised to want a car so badly that you can't walk away from a deal.

Insurance and Extended Warranties

Automobile insurance, to cover damage to your car, another person's car, another person or their property, or yourself, is a big annual expense for many people. In some states, auto insurance prices are regulated, and the premiums don't vary much from one company to another. In other states, however, the premiums do vary. The key considerations are cost and how good the company's reputation is for paying a claim if you have a problem. Magazines like *Consumer Reports* run specific surveys on these matters, too. A good, general-purpose insurance agent may be able to help you find the best auto policy.

One way to hold down your auto insurance costs is to take the highest deductible possible on the coverage you have to have. A deductible is similar to a copayment to a doctor at an HMO—it's the amount you pay, or your financial share of any claim. For example, you might have a copayment of $5 on doctor's visits on your medical policy. On your automobile policy, you might agree to pay for the first $200 of repair bills if someone dents the fender of your car while it's parked. That's the deductible. If you get a higher deductible, say $500, then your premiums for the rest of the coverage will be lower. But you're taking the risk that if something happens, you'll have $500 in an emergency savings account to cover the damage. Insurance is all about risk and timing of events. That's why it helps to look at your spending plan with these factors in mind. Over time, for example, you might be able to build up enough of a car emergency fund to justify taking a higher deductible.

Another way to lower your auto insurance costs is to eliminate any coverage you're not required to have. When a car is still under a loan agreement, for example, your lender may require you pay for collision coverage for repairs if you get hit, but you can drop this coverage when the car is paid for. Older cars that have declined in value may really not be worth the cost of collision coverage.

Other ways to lower your driving insurance costs are to keep clean driving records and to install antitheft devices in the car, even a simple lock around the steering wheel. Another option is to join an auto club that will make you eligible for a discount on your premiums.

So far, all this talk about auto insurance has focused on protecting you in case of an accident, a theft, or a tree falling on your car. Another form of insurance available on cars nowadays is called an extended warranty. These warranties are sold—not given away—to protect you against the costs of mechanical problems that may show up later. Is an extended warranty worth the cost? It may not be. If you're buying a car with a good record for reliability, have had it checked by a mechanic, and think you're making the right decision, why not put the money toward savings that could be used for a variety of emergencies, instead of paying for insurance that will be specific to repairing your car under certain guidelines? It's a judgment call in each situation, but don't automatically let yourself be talked into paying for an extended warranty.

Regular Maintenance

Keeping your car in good working order and investing a little here and there in its maintenance can prevent both financial and automotive disasters. The standard advice is to change the oil every 3,000 miles to keep your engine in good repair and keep it running for a long time, although some newer cars are designed to go longer between oil changes. Keep the tires inflated properly (read the owner's manual) to get the best mileage. Do what you can to protect your car against rust, such as cleaning road salt from it if you live in snowy areas, cleaning out moisture around the bottoms of the door casings, and sanding down small rust spots and covering them with paint primer and paint made specifically for that purpose (available in discount and auto parts stores).

Avoid spending too much money on gasoline. AAA says that in 1996, Americans wasted $1.7 billion on premium gasoline that wouldn't make their cars run any better than regular. Less than 10 percent of the cars on the road actually need premium gasoline, according to AAA, and they tend to be those with high-performance engines and some sport-utility vehicles. But other cars on the road that don't knock or ping when they're filled up with regular gasoline aren't going to get better mileage, power, performance, or cleaner fuel burning from premium gasoline, according to AAA.

Action Items

Invest enough in your car so it can safely and reliably transport you—not so you can make a fashion statement.

Shop around for the best insurance rates, financing deals, auto club memberships, and gasoline prices.

Consolidate your trips and errands to save time and car expenses. Car pool when you can.

Action Items

(Continued)

If you finish paying off a car loan, apply that monthly payment amount to another savings goal, such as money for the next car you'll need, or to pay off some other bills, or to create an emergency fund.

....

Know the terms of any loans you take out, especially if there is any penalty for paying off the car early. Stay abreast of interest rates; some people have been able to refinance their car loans at lower rates when interest rates have fallen.

....

Keep up with any mileage reimbursement policies from your employer so that you can get compensated if you need to use your car for work.

Chapter 10

Housing

Shelter costs are likely to be the
biggest part of your expenses, and having the right kind of housing will play a big part
in your happiness. So it's important to get the right balance of a good place to live and
a reasonable fix on your housing costs.

It's likely that you're going to be renting for awhile, whether that means you have your
own apartment, or share a place with roommates. If you live with your family for awhile,
you may be expected to pay room and board, or some of the household expenses.

The tricky part of understanding housing expenses when you're first starting out is
taking into account all the factors and expenses you'll encounter. It's more than just
the obvious issue of rent, which will be determined by supply and demand, how close
the dwelling is to business and employment districts, shopping, and transportation, the
attractiveness of the apartment, and the safety of the neighborhood.

Utilities, such as phone, electricity, heat and hot water, cable, parking, and so on
will all add to your housing costs. Even if some services are included in the rent, such
as heat, you can be sure that your rent is set at a level to compensate the landlord, so

you really are paying for the heat, although indirectly. There are a couple of ways to find out how much it's really going to cost you to live in a particular place. One is to ask the landlord, previous tenants, or any roommates about their experience with utilities. You can also call the utility companies and ask, for example, for the history of electric costs at a given address. Meanwhile, ask the utility companies about any budget plans they have that might save you money or help you predict your costs more accurately. Utilities also generally offer advice on ways to cut down on energy usage, such as tips on reducing heating costs or ways to cut down on your need for air-conditioning. Ask what types of free consumer advice or audits they have to offer, and incorporate their suggestions into your living space.

A related cost of housing is insurance—even for renters. If a fire destroyed your apartment building, for example, your landlord would likely have coverage to cover the loss of the structure. But your possessions, such as the clothing you wear to work, your stereo, or your computer, wouldn't be covered by that insurance if they are lost in a fire. You also need insurance in case any of your belongings are stolen. There are two kinds of insurance you can buy: a policy that will cover the costs of replacing the items you lost, or a policy that will cover the cash value of the items. It's really wiser to get the first type, that will give you replacement costs, even though this type of policy is more expensive. For example, if you lost your work clothes in a fire and you only had the cash value coverage, the insurance company would likely tell you that your used shirts and underwear weren't worth much, that your suits, slacks, dresses, or skirts had little value, and that your outerwear didn't hold a high value either. Yet, to go out and replace all those things so that you could go back to work in appropriate attire could costs you hundreds of dollars, and you might end up putting that on a credit card. That's why having the replacement cost, which would give you enough money to get new clothing, is more advantageous.

To get the best deal, you should talk to a few insurance agents or companies and compare prices. If you have a car, ask whether the coverage is cheaper if you buy policies for both items from the same company. Also ask about getting discounts for any security or alarm, features that are in the home, whether it's a deadbolt lock, a fire/smoke alarm or a more sophisticated security system.

Getting the policy is really only half the job of protecting your belongings, however. To establish what you lost to the insurance company, you'd have to have a list or an inventory of your belongings. You can do this on paper (see the inventory worksheet later in this chapter) or with a software program. You need to store at least one copy of the inventory, whether it's on paper or on a disk, away from home. If your house goes up in flames, after all, it won't do you any good to have the inventory if that burns too. If you can store a personal file in a desk at work, that would be one option, although in some settings it's really not good to keep personal belongings at your work area. Another idea would be for you and a friend to swap copies of inventories. There are also some fireproof safes on the market, but off-site storage is better. Some people rent safe deposit boxes at banks to hold these and other valuable belongings and important documents, and prefer to pay the bank charges.

Insurance Information Institute, Inc.
A nonprofit action and information center

TAKING INVENTORY

Should you ever need to report a burglary or file an insurance claim...a household inventory could be a valuable document.

PORCH/PATIO

Article & Description	Purchase Date	Purchase Price
Chairs		
Tables		
Umbrella		
Floor covering		
Lamps		
Outdoor cooking equipment		
Plants/planters		
Other		
Total		

Home Inventory Worksheet provided by The Insurance Information Institute

WHY TAKE INVENTORY?

Try this test. Sit in your kitchen and make a list of everything in your living room. No peeking!

Now—check on how many items you missed.

No one really expects to lose furniture or other belongings in a fire, a burglary or a tornado. But such events do occur. If disaster struck your home, would you be able to report exactly what you lost to police, to the IRS, or to your insurance company?

An up-to-date inventory of your household furnishings and personal belongings can help to:
● Determine the value of your belongings and your personal insurance needs.
● Establish the purchase dates and cost of major items in case of a loss.
● Identify exactly what was lost (most people can't recall items accumulated gradually).
● Settle your insurance claim quickly and efficiently.
● Verify losses for income tax deductions.

START RIGHT AWAY!

Use the form in this folder to get started on your inventory.

List major items in each room. Note serial numbers (usually found on the bottom or the back of major appliances), purchase prices, present value and dates of purchase where possible. Attach any available receipts.

Ask your insurance representative to assist you if you have questions or concerns.

Remember—the more thorough your inventory, the more valuable it will be in case of a loss.

To back up your written inventory, photograph each wall of each room with closet or cabinet doors open. On the back of each picture, write the date, the general location and contents shown.

Store your inventory and photographs in a safe place away from home.

Keep a copy of the inventory and negatives of the photographs at home so that you can update your inventory from time to time.

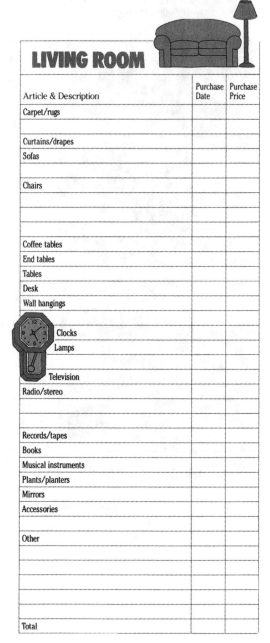

Article & Description	Purchase Date	Purchase Price
LIVING ROOM		
Carpet/rugs		
Curtains/drapes		
Sofas		
Chairs		
Coffee tables		
End tables		
Tables		
Desk		
Wall hangings		
Clocks		
Lamps		
Television		
Radio/stereo		
Records/tapes		
Books		
Musical instruments		
Plants/planters		
Mirrors		
Accessories		
Other		
Total		

DINING ROOM

Article & Description	Purchase Date	Purchase Price
Carpet/rugs		
Curtains/drapes		
Buffet		
Tables		
Chairs		
China cabinet		
China		
Silverware		
Glassware		
Clocks		
Lamps/fixtures		
Wall hangings		
Serving table/cart		
Other		
Total		

BATHROOM

Clothes hamper		
Curtains		
Dressing table		
Electrical appliances		
Scale		
Shower curtains		
Linens		
Other		
Total		

KITCHEN

Article & Description	Purchase Date	Purchase Price
Tables		
Chairs		
Curtains		
Cabinets		
Lighting fixtures		
Bowls		
Pots/pans		
Utensils		
Cutlery		
Dishes		
Refrigerator		
Stove		
Dishwasher		
Disposal unit		
Freezer		
Washer		
Dryer		
Small appliances		
Clocks		
Radios		
Step stool		
Food/supplies		
Other		
Total		

BEDROOMS

Article & Description	Purchase Date	Purchase Price
Bookcases		
Chairs		
Carpet/rugs		
Curtains/drapes		
Beds		
Mattresses		
Cedar chest		
Desk		
Dressers		
Dressing tables		
Night tables		
Lamps		
Mirrors		
Clocks		
Radios		
Sewing machine		
Television		
Toilet articles		
Wall hangings		
Clothing		
Other		
Total		

GARAGE/BASEMENT/ATTIC

Article & Description	Purchase Date	Purchase Price
Furniture		
Luggage/trunks		
Sports equipment		
Toys		
Outdoor games		
Ornamental lawn items		
Lawn mower		
Shovels		
Spreaders		
Sprinklers/hoses		
Wheelbarrow		
Snow blower		
Garden tools/supplies		
Ladders/step stools		
Work bench		
Carpentry tools/supplies		
Canned goods/supplies		
Pet supplies		
Other		
Total		

Rent or Buy?

The old assumption was that eventually everyone would want to buy some sort of housing, whether it was an apartment in a cooperatively owned building, a condo, a single-family home, or a two-or-more family home that you could live in and rent out the rest. Recently, that wisdom has been questioned, and some people find it better simply to rent. They don't want the upkeep, property taxes, and added headaches of having a home. Or they're not so sure they'll still be in the same place in the next two years if a better job offer comes along, so it just doesn't seem worth it to commit. That said, lots of people do eventually want to buy their own place. Even though they would have to pay a down payment, finance the rest of the purchase with a mortgage loan, and have monthly mortgage payments for 20 or 30 years, they like being able to do whatever they want to the house, and look forward to the day when the mortgage will be fully paid, and their cost of living will drop.

That's what has propelled so many people in recent years—you may recall this happening in your family—to get mortgages at cheaper rates when interest rates fell, which made the required monthly payments smaller. Some people used the cash they saved for other purposes, but many people found it a good opportunity to gain total ownership of the house faster. With the lower interest rates, they were able to put more money toward paying off the house faster, because the financing was cheaper. Any time you can get cheaper financing on a house, then you can apply the saved money to the principal of the loan, which refers to the actual purchase price of the house (or a car, in auto loans). That gets you the house faster, and over time saves you money. The findings are that mortgaging a house triples its cost because of the interest costs over the years. This is one way banks make money. The bank knows people don't have the tens of thousands of dollars it takes to buy a house outright, so they will go to the bank for financing.

If Buying Is a Goal

If you do want to buy a home some day, one of your first steps should be to start saving now for a down payment. The most traditional way to buy a home has been to come up with a down payment of 20 percent of the purchase price, and to finance the other 80 percent through a mortgage. So, if you were buying a home for $100,000, you'd pay $20,000, get a bank loan for $80,000, and make monthly mortgage payments to the bank.

As housing prices have increased over the years, it's been harder and harder for young people to come up with that 20 percent, even with years of saving or investing. That doesn't mean you shouldn't save, although. The best thing to do is to save specifically for a down payment, and as you get ready to look into buying a house, look for programs that will let you finance with what you can afford. For example, some banks may let you buy a house for 10 percent down, although there may be other requirements put on you, such as buying insurance to cover the lender if you default on the mortgage payment (Private Mortgage Insurance or PMI). Other programs that banks or housing agencies may offer, especially to first-time home buyers, can have lower requirements for down payments. Or, they may try to make it easier to come up with the down payment in other ways. In 1996, for example, the Federal Housing Authority started a program that would let family and friends contribute money to a formal savings program for newlyweds to gather a house down payment. (Call 1-800-CALL FHA if you're interested.)

It's important to keep in mind that you still have to come up with the money for the monthly mortgage payments, and if your down payment is too small, that would tend to increase the size of your monthly payments. But in the past several years, lots of people have realized they could have been making monthly mortgage payments equivalent to what they were paying in rent. The big obstacle has been in figuring out how to come up with the down payment to get into the door, and that's why there are more programs looking at these issues.

To take a broader look at the situation, though, you can go to a lender and ask them to *prequalify* you for a loan. That means they'll look at your income and savings and see how big a loan you could realistically handle. In essence, they can tell you how expensive a house you can purchase, or if you can't qualify, what you could change in your financial situation to make yourself a more attractive borrowing customer. Bear in mind, you don't have to go out and get absolutely the most expensive dwelling youcan possibly afford. Naturally, it's better not to do that, and to settle into something you can afford comfortably. When you first move in, you may literally spend hundreds on curtains, wallpaper, and paint, even if it takes you a few years to add major furnishings. Further, you'll find it better to have that financial flexibility that lower home payments will give you for routine maintenance, property insurance you'll need, taxes, and savings.

Figuring Out What You Need and Want

There are lots of ways to buy housing these days. You can go through the traditional route and talk to a real estate salesperson who is representing several sellers. They can show you houses that their clients are looking to sell, but remember, their first obligation is the client's best interests, not yours. In some areas, brokers are now available who represent the buyers and help them find a house, for a fee, of course. In other instances, you may run across someone who wants to sell their house privately, one-on-one, without a broker involved. Advertisements, driving around, checking bulletin boards, watching local television programming, and screening homes via computer records at a real estate office are all ways that you can get a feel for what kind of housing is available where you are. You might also consider looking at some of the less-conventional options in housing, such as:

- Co-housing communities that provide individual units but also some common areas and activities.

- Building kits that you and friends can assemble into a home, or alternate building designs, such as straw bale housing that uses dried straw packed in a frame to create an energy-efficient home.

- Modular homes that buyers select from a range of designs, and that builders assemble from premanufactured pieces.

Whatever your situation is, you'll find that you save a lot of time and aggravation if you narrow and specify your preferences as much as possible. For example, how many bedrooms do you need? Would it be okay to have one bathroom instead of two—two might be a want, but not a need. Do you want a yard for a garden, or would you rather not have the bother? Does anybody need a separate room away from the living quarters for quiet work? Do you need to live on one floor? Are there any particular styles that you like or would absolutely rule out, whether it's a colonial or ranch? These are core questions that will determine what houses are even worth looking at. Other questions that deal with more temporal or cosmetic questions, such as the color of the wallpaper in the living room, don't belong here. That situation can be changed and dealt with later.

Another big consideration, especially for young people trying to get into a house for the least amount of money possible, is how much work they're willing to do on a house that has seen better days. Home repair can be costly and time-consuming, so some people would rule out any dwellings that needed major work. But other people like the challenge of working on home projects, have the skills, can get the tools, and can save some money in the bargain. The trick is in distinguishing between which houses are the bargains, and which houses will endlessly suck away your future earnings in repairs that never seem to stop. Home Depot, a store that provides home improvement materials, says there are ways consumers can tell the difference. A good "fixer-upper" will have a good solid foundation and suffer mostly cosmetic mishaps, while a nightmare needs fundamental repair to the major home systems.

Good potential	Peeling paint, old carpet, or bad landscaping are problems that can easily and relatively inexpensively be fixed to give you a more attractive and valuable home.
Bad potential	Inspectors you hire before the sale find the home needs to have heating or plumbing or electrical systems replaced, or the roof leaks, or the foundation is shaky, or on an eroding piece of property.

Bear in mind that kitchens and bathrooms are the among the rooms most apt to be renovated in a house because they improve the functioning of the home and add value to the house. But it's not wise financially to improve a house so much that if you wanted to sell it, it would be much more expensive than other homes in the neighborhood. A substantially higher price ticket could eliminate your home from the market in many buyer's minds.

The Mechanics of Home Purchasing

There's an elaborate, although orderly, set of procedures involved in the house-buying transaction. It's best not to worry about this too much, because you have real estate salespeople, a lawyer for yourself, and a bank looking over the process. In simplified terms, you find a house you like, find out the price being asked, and make an offer to buy through the real estate salesperson. Your offer will be contingent on getting inspections and having everything check out okay. The buyer either likes the price you offered or doesn't, and you either make another offer on this property, or start again on another one.

When there's an agreement on the price, the property is inspected, property records are checked, your lawyer looks over the agreement, and a "closing date" is scheduled when you go to the bank, pick up the keys, and get ready to move in. This is a hectic time full of errands, but the big financial implication of all this activity comes down to two words: closing costs. It can cost $1,000 or more just to get all the paperwork taken care of and fees paid to complete a housing deal. (See the following chart.) So that's extra money you don't have for the down payment or for monthly mortgage payments. It's hard to get around, but sometimes a seller will offer to pay part of the closing costs to sweeten the deal. You can also shop around the different lenders to see which offers the best overall deal, including closing costs.

TYPICAL CLOSING COSTS INVOLVED IN A HOME PURCHASE

- Fees, called points, that are paid back to the lender, with 1 point being equal to 1 percent of the principal of the loan

- Private mortgage insurance

- Legal fees, including for the bank's attorney

- Title search, which checks property records before a sale to make sure the property can be legally sold and that there are no other claims on it

- Title insurance, which protects the lender from any financial mishaps if there is some kind of mistake in the title ownership records

- Recording fees to cover the costs of recording the mortgage and the deed at your local government level

- Other fees for miscellaneous services

Action Items

Be aware of how much different housing costs would be if you changed your commute slightly, say 15 minutes in either direction. If you cut your housing costs, would your transportation costs go up, and by how much, or, if you cut your commute, would your housing costs increase? Factor the information into your spending plan.

....

If you have roommates, agree to check in with them regularly to discuss house finances, to make sure agreements are operating fairly and smoothly, and to find out if there are any ways of saving money.

....

Before moving into an apartment, have the landlord acknowledge in writing—maybe in a note on the lease agreement—any damage that already exists in the apartment so that you won't be charged for it when you leave. Examples might be a dent in a wall or a door, or a cracked pane of glass.

....

Make sure there are adequate locks on the doors—deadbolts are generally the best—and if needed, on the windows. Find out if the landlord would be willing to install these items if they're not currently in place. Talk to your police station or community law enforcement authority to find out what they say about the relative safety of your neighborhood, and any suggestions they have for improving security.

....

Update your home inventory every year, or when you make a major purchase.

....

If owning a house is your dream, have a picture of the type of house you'd like to have where you can see it, to remind you of this savings goal. Don't invest too much in furnishing, decorating, or landscaping rental properties you live in along the way, because those purchases might not transfer to your home. The year before you're ready to jump into the home-buying market, start educating yourself gradually about its workings by paying attention to advertisements, articles on real estate, and visiting home shows. Ask for references of real estate salespeople from trusted friends.

Chapter 11

Moving

Moving can be exciting, or it can be an expensive and aggravating proposition, but it's largely unavoidable. You might need to move a few times in the next decade, as a matter of fact, not only to get into better housing, but because of a job move or personal reasons. And you'll likely be asked to help friends who are doing the same.

The first few times you move, out of a parent's home or a college room, or an apartment, the stakes aren't so high. You might be able to transport things in a couple of carloads, especially if you're only going across town. But as you go further, and acquire more furniture, you'll probably need to incur some transportation costs. You might want to rent a van or a small truck, for example, or ship some of your belongings to your new address. Eventually, you might even hire movers for a move into a bigger apartment, a house, or to a new job.

Set the Stage

Anybody who has packed a few times will tell you that less is better. Before you even start packing, go through your closets, your basement, your cupboards, and set aside anything you don't want or need to take with you. Give it away, sell it at a yard sale, or donate it to charity. If you have to pack it, it will just consume more of your time and supplies. If movers pack it or transport it, it's more of their time and more weight on the load.

Use up the food you have to avoid spoilage and waste, and try to pack meals or some food for your road trip.

Going the Do-It-Yourself Route

If you're going to use or procure your own supplies, do your own packing, and your own driving and hauling, you will save money. As a matter of fact, do-it-yourself moves can cost as much as 80 percent less than using professional movers. Ryder Consumer Truck Rentals did a study in January 1996 and found that for moves up to 500 miles, the costs came to an average of $511 for people who handled it themselves, or 27 percent of the $1,834 spent on the average by people who used commercial movers. It will take time and planning though, and you have to make sure you can afford that, or can get help from friends and family.

First, focus on the supplies. You can save money by asking grocery stores, bookstores, or liquor stores if you can have the boxes that they are going to discard. Start asking early and stopping in often to make sure that you get enough boxes, because you don't know which stores will let you have boxes, what days they'll get shipments, when they'll have empty boxes ready for you, and so on. You can also buy materials at shipping companies and truck rental outfits, but the supplies there can be costly, unless you can get recycled boxes. Wardrobe boxes, for example, can be used again and again, and make it easy to transport the contents of a closet from one place to another.

Be careful how you pack the boxes—both to save the contents and to make the boxes easy to lift. (See the figure on the following page.) Don't try to save money by overpacking boxes or by skimping on tape. You'll pay for it later in broken belongings and regrets. Keep a running inventory of what you're packing, label the contents of the boxes clearly, and label the destination as specifically as possible. Even if you're moving into a studio apartment, it will make things easier on arrival if one box is labeled "Alarm clock/phone/lamp for bedside" and another box of the same dimensions is marked "kitchen utensils and coffee pot."

If you're renting a truck or van, try to describe how much you'll be moving as accurately as possible to the rental representative so that you can rent the right-sized van or truck. The bigger the vehicle is, the more you'll have to pay, so be careful. But it's better to rent something a little bigger than you need, than to rent a vehicle that's too small and have to make more than one trip. A small, 10-foot truck might be enough to

How to Pack and Label a Box

Wrap fragile items in several layers of newsprint to protect them. Use tissue paper for porcelain or china, since newsprint can stain these items. Try to keep the weight of each box under 30 pounds.

Grouping items of similar purpose in the same box helps eliminate confusion when unpacking. For instance, pack a box of kitchen accessories that you'll need as soon as you arrive. That way, you'll have enough dishes, pots and pans for the first meal in your new home.

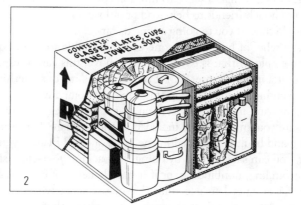

Use a thick felt-tip pen to label each box with a list of contents and the room in which it belongs and mark which side should be placed up. Put a priority number on each box to speed unpacking. High priority items include kitchen equipment, clothing and cleaning and bathroom supplies.

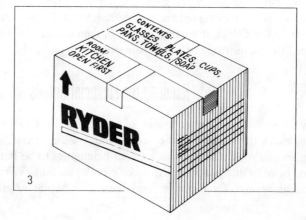

haul one or two rooms of belongings, but it's hard to visualize how things might fit into different-sized trucks on your first experience moving.

Compare prices from different truck rental companies, and if you have any flexibility in your schedule at all, ask them on what days of the week they offer the best rates. The cost of truck rental varies with supply and demand, and you might get a better price midweek than on a Saturday, and in the middle of the month, as compared to the last week in the month.

When you get to your new place, unload the truck and return it. Don't start unpacking until you return the rental truck. If you are renting by the hour, it will cost more to unpack as you unload because you'll be slowed down.

On your way back to the rental truck outlet, replenish the gasoline tank with the least expensive fuel possible. That way you'll avoid refueling charges at the truck rental outlet, which will charge more than the price of gasoline that you buy.

Hiring a Professional

Even though you may not have much to move, and the costs are higher, there may still be times when it makes sense to hire someone. For example, if you're by yourself, and can't get enough friends to help load or unload a truck for you, you might want a company to do that. If you're going a long distance, say more than a day's drive, you might want the relief of having someone else responsible for transporting the goods. If you have an employer that is paying for your move, this can be especially attractive (more on that later in the chapter). Or if you have a piano, or something else that really needs special handling, you'll have to find the right company.

The moving industry advises you to get estimates from two or three movers, and make sure you know what is included in the estimate. For example, is just hauling, or packing and hauling included in the price quoted? Even if you're using a professional mover, you can save money by doing the packing yourself. Ask the mover if the estimate is binding, nonbinding, or if it has elements of each. Ask if the price would be better if you agreed to a certain day of the week when it's not peak time for the company. After you select the mover, make sure that you've made yourself a list of everything they're picking up, and double-check that list when they drop off the items. Ask how to file a claim if anything is lost or damaged, and then file a claim quickly if you need to; the moving company has insurance to cover this.

Handling the Financial Details

To pay for a move, you can generally use a cashier's check or a credit card, though you need to check the terms with the vendor you're using. If you have an employer that's paying for you to rent a truck, or for your belongings to be hauled, that's great news. But you have to find out what the specific policy is: Some companies may give you a moving allowance, for example, and have you decide whether to spend it on a professional company, or on a rental truck you're willing to drive so that you can take any leftover cash and apply it toward expenses for your new home. Make sure you keep all your receipts for moving if you're relocating 50 miles away from your present job: If you have to pay for a truck or a mover yourself, you may be able to deduct that cost on your income tax, even if you don't itemize your deductions. You can't deduct the expenses for just going to another place to check out apartments or houses, however. If you've got an employer who picks up the tab for those kinds of costs, be careful, because the current tax law considers those reimbursements to be income and you will be taxed when you file your federal income taxes.

Action Items

Figure out as closely as you can how your cost of living will be different in your new place. Even in you're only moving 20 miles, the housing prices, for example, may be different. If you're moving farther away, look at information from the local chamber of commerce, local media, and any available magazine rankings or online data for an idea of the cost of living, so you can work on a spending plan that fits your new circumstances. Companies that offer services on this topic are Runzheimer International at 1-800-558-1702, and Right Choice Inc. at 1-800-872-2294, which also has a software package.

Get a brochure about moving from your post office so you can send out change of address cards before you move.

Make a checklist and make sure all utilities, lights, water, heat, and so on will be available when you get to your new home.

If you're moving to a new area, get set up as quickly as possible with a new checking account and any other bank accounts you need. Have a reserve of traveler's checks if there's going to be a lapse in time between active bank accounts.

If you're moving to a new state and have a car, find out what you have to do to get it registered and your driver's license switched over.

Chapter 12

Saving and Investing

In many of the books on personal
finance, advice on saving and investing is presented in early chapters. Right off the bat,
readers are told what to do to accumulate more money, and saving early and often is
certainly good advice.

The previous chapters in this book have concentrated more on earning, handling,
and spending cash, because for a few years after college, young adults frequently stay in
the mode of acquiring things for their developing households. Saving money may not
be as attractive as doing things with money as soon as you get your hands on it.

TIDBIT: The standard advice is to save 10 percent of your income, but many Americans only save only 4 or
5 percent.

But, now it's time to reckon with the fact that saving and investing will always be important, all your life. You might as well get into the habit now, if you're not already.

The Difference Between Saving and Investing

Think about putting money away for different kinds of purposes. Focusing on a specific use, such as a down payment on a house, keeps you more clearly concentrated on your goals, and more motivated. If you're accumulating capital for something in particular, you're not as apt to feel that you're being deprived of that money for immediate spending. Distinguishing between different purposes and outcomes will also help you decide how to handle various sums of money.

Savings can be thought of as money that you need to have access to, not for things that happen every week, but for events that could happen at any time. For example, the refrigerator breaks down and all the food you just bought is spoiled. It's helpful to have some household savings set aside for a situation like that, or for car emergencies, for example.

It's good to have a larger sum of money set aside elsewhere as an emergency fund in case of job loss. Financial advisers usually suggest having three to six months' worth of living expenses set aside. As people move higher up in their fields of endeavor, sometimes it may take them six months or a year to find a job comparable to one that was lost—there are usually more entry-level jobs open than senior-level posts. That means growing more of a cushion. This money should be available where you can get it readily. You wouldn't want to have it in a certificate of deposit, because you might need it before the certificate matures, and then you would lose some of the money to a penalty. Still, you don't want it in your regular checking account where it can get sucked up by day-to-day expenses. Find a savings vehicle devoted just to this. Don't expect to earn much interest on this money, because your main priority is to have it accessible when you need it, not to produce income of its own.

Investing, on the other hand, can be thought of as the art and science of getting some money working to replicate itself. Life would be easier if people could earn enough from their jobs to set aside money in simple savings situations for all their future needs. Unfortunately, the contemporary world doesn't work that way. Not only do you have to work, a portion of the money you earn has to be set to work in investment vehicles suited to creating more money for specific, more distant purposes. Such purposes might be getting enough money for a down payment for a house, buying a business, or funding your retirement through a company-sponsored plan, Individual Retirement Account, or other ways.

Sometimes people think investing is only for those who are already rich. But in reality, if you work in a career with modest pay, it's especially important for you to start investing early. Time is the element you've got on your side, so you want to use that to your maximum advantage. By investing even small sums, you can build up substantial accumulations over the years as the value of the investments themselves increase. And if your pay is meager, you probably won't be able to save enough simply from earnings stashed away at low interest rates to handle all your life's projects. Women should also keep in mind that they have historically earned less than men, and you want to get what money you do make to work extra hard to help compensate for any gender-pay gap. This is also true if you plan on taking any time off from your regular income-producing schedule to devote time to family needs, child care, or personal interests.

Mutual Fund Investing

For most people with active careers and other interests, mutual funds have proven to be the best way to invest. Mutual funds are not insured—even when sold by banks—so there is some risk of losing the money that you put into a fund. But if you don't invest, you'll lose money as inflation erodes the value of cash. And holding onto investments over time diminishes the chances of losing money, as the investments get the opportunity to grow. So investing is necessary, and *mutual funds* are the way in. Mutual funds let you into the investing world for relatively small sums of money, and let you have a far greater sampling of investing opportunities than would be available if you tried to spend a modest sum, of say $1,000, on direct shares in companies (stocks) or bonds. Bonds are like loans: Investors forward a government authority or a company money, and the authority or the company issues a bond to the investors. The borrower has to pay the investor back in a scheduled time period with interest. The bond matures when the loan comes due. People can buy and sell bonds that have been issued, but haven't yet matured, but then the value fluctuates depending on interest rates. Mutual funds, because of their size and breadth, can invest in numerous companies, or numerous bond offerings. Individual investors buy shares in the mutual fund, and that way get indirect access to the stocks or bonds held by the fund. Simply put, it's a way the middle-class person can participate in the wealth of building new companies, markets for products, and government projects like airports and roads. The fund manager is the person responsible for making the investing decisions and staying on top of what stocks or bonds the fund should buy or sell at any given time. This working arrangement takes a lot of pressure off the small investor, who wouldn't have time to monitor all these decisions weekly or daily.

TIDBIT: Twelve percent of mutual fund shareholders are between ages 18 to 30, according to a survey in 1996 by the Investment Company Institute. The Generation X investors in the study typically were 28 years old, college graduates, working, married, and living in a household with a $50,000 annual income. The typical Generation X investor also had $6,000 invested in three funds—all from one company—and showed more tolerance for investment risk than other generations.

There are some important consumer aspects to consider when buying funds. The first thing you might think of is the going price of the shares on the market, technically called the Net Asset Value, or NAV in performance listings. Still, it may be more useful to you to set aside a certain amount each month, $50 or more, to automatically invest in your desired funds. If the NAV is down in a particular month, fine, your money will buy more shares. If the price is up, your sum will buy fewer shares. But you won't worry so much about short-term variations because with this system—called dollar cost averaging—you're getting the comfort of knowing you're making regular contributions to your investing goals. Time will be your ally in allowing the money to grow over the long term, and you're taking care of the most important consideration—habitually adding to your investment portfolio, even if the monthly sums are small.

A related question in the price area are the fees funds charge to the investor. The fees pay salaries and other costs of running the funds. Basically, there can be:

- Low-load funds that keep sales fees to a minimum

- Load funds that charge a sales fee either when you purchase into the fund, or if you sell the fund shares within a certain period of time

- Annual charges for management

- Specific marketing fees called 12b-1 fees

The more you spend in fees, the less cash you have for investing. But you also needn't be too preoccupied with charges—which are detailed in the legal document, the prospectus, that describes the fund. For one thing, you don't want to get so caught up in sorting out charges that you never invest—analysis paralysis. Secondly, like shopping for anything else, you want value from your mutual fund. You want to buy the best financial performance, and sometimes you may get that from a load fund—even after you've accounted for the charges. The low-load fund industry will tell you that there's such a wide variety of funds available now that for any load fund you like, you can probably find a low-load fund to substitute for it. But if you're buying funds from a professional who charges a fee (more on that later), you can also put good consumerism to use: Ask if you're getting all the advice and services that the fee covers. Ask if there's a better time or way to pay the fee—maybe an upfront fee, for example, isn't right for you. With these questions in mind, you can sort out which funds look the best to you for their investments and their value.

The more fundamental questions for most mutual fund investors surround the different categories of funds in this big market, and what level of risk corresponds to each of these categories. One way to look at risk is: How much can you stand? The payoff for taking more risk is that you might get a bigger return on your money in years to come. If you take a smaller risk, you're likely to get a more modest but more predictable sum back, which is often helpful in financial planning. Another way to consider risk is: What do you want to accomplish, and how soon will you need the money? If you're 26, for example, and investing for retirement in 40 years, you can afford to look at some riskier mutual funds because if you hit a stumbling block 10 years down the road, you'll still have 30 more years to recoup and make more progress. On the other hand, if you've got some money set aside to enroll in graduate school in a couple of years, you want that money in a fund that's more stable in its price and growth records. That's because you've got a specific, near-term goal in mind, and you don't want to chance that the market will take a slide and temporarily erode the value of your mutual fund during just the week you were going to sell the shares and use the money for your tuition payment. If over the past 10 years or so your parents were simultaneously investing for their retirement and your college tuition, they faced the same timing questions. Generally, people solve these questions of multiple needs by taking their investment money and dividing into different risk classifications, depending on when they need the money and how fast and how much they want it to grow. The categories are usually described in the following, or similar, terms:

- *Aggressive growth funds.* These are funds that are invested in companies that pay little if anything in dividends—checks to shareholders now funded from earnings the company makes. But because these companies are growing and expected to be successful, the value of their shares will also presumably grow over the years, and they'll pay more in dividends. That way the investor could sell the shares later for much more than the purchase price.

- *Growth funds.* These funds also look for companies that still have room to expand in their fields, but aren't as apt to go for companies that are as small, youthful, or risky as aggressive growth funds.

- *International and/or global.* At least some of the money in these funds is invested in stocks or bonds from companies outside the United States. The thinking is that some developing economies may have more room to grow than the United States economy, or that if the U.S. economy is flat at any one point, the fortunes of another country's industry might be improving. The terms "international" and "global" are used in different ways by different fund companies, so investors in each case have to be careful to understand whether a fund invests partially in the United States and partially outside, or whether it invests all its money abroad.

- *Income funds.* Income funds usually provide investors with shares in companies that are well-established corporations known for steadily paying cash dividends. That way, the investor is always getting a stream of money from the company.

- *Growth and income funds.* This type of fund combines the major aspects of the growth and income funds. This category is also similar to something called a balanced fund, which may have some investments in bonds.

- *Bond funds.* These funds invest just in bonds, but probably on staggered timetables of maturity. The bonds can either be from companies or government authorities. Bond funds are meant to provide income, but can still carry some investment risk.

There are also other ways to categorize funds; for example, by specialty. These funds may concentrate on one sector, like the environment or metals, or they may be socially responsible funds that try to invest in companies that meet not only financial standards, but certain standards of conduct. Depending on the fund, the manager may stay away from companies that produce tobacco, firearms, or that have many environmental or workforce management problems. Funds might also have some kind of tax-saving objective that's plowed into the name. These classifications can all be piled on top of each other; for example, a global, socially responsible growth fund. Don't let the lingo scare you, just pick the adjectives apart one by one and ask if you don't know what they mean, and also what they mean when they're all combined.

The younger you are, the more likely you've got more of your investment money in growth or aggressive funds for retirement. Retired people are more likely to be using bond funds because they're not earning large or regular paychecks anymore, but need steady income for household expenses. A young person might have some money in a bond fund for awhile if a big event like a house down payment is coming up in a few weeks, and it's important to shield that money from any dips in the stock market until the house deal is signed. One of the problems mutual fund investors have run into recently is that funds aren't always invested the way they're described. The managers in charge may actually be taking more risk than you want, for example. Read the prospectus, find out what the funds invest in, and look at what kinds of returns they expect to get, or have gotten in the past.

If you're researching mutual funds on your own, a way to shortcut the process is to look at a guide like *Morningstar*, which rates mutual funds. This information can often be found in libraries, and is frequently quoted in the financial news media. Past performance of a mutual fund isn't going to assure you of what will happen in the future, but it will let you know something about how well the managers have fared. A prospectus describes the fund and its objectives, just as a prospectus can describe a company that is selling shares of stock. It's dry stuff, but you really do need to read it.

Mutual funds are sold in banks (although they're not insured, as bank deposits are), through brokerage houses, directly from fund companies, by discount brokerage houses, online, and through financial professionals like certified financial planners and chartered financial analysts. If you want to work with a financial adviser, the best idea is to ask around for references and talk to some of them before you decide. You'll want someone you trust, with whom you can honestly discuss your lifestyle, and who also may be able to give you references to other professionals you may need from time to time, such as accountants or attorneys. The Institute of Certified Financial Planners operates a referral line (1-800-282-7526) that gives consumers names of planners in their area. Find out how planners charge for their services, because some of them may get commissions for selling financial and investment products as part of their compensation. Some consumers believe that impairs the adviser's objectivity, although others don't mind because they are actively helping select their own investment products to purchase, and feel the commission keeps the consumer's fee down. The other option is that financial advisers charge the client a fee, or a combination of a client fee and commission.

Using Employer Savings Plans

Much of your investing life will be made easier if your employer offers a 401(k) plan, or one of its counterparts, that lets you put pretax money away to invest for retirement. You select what percentage of your gross pay is deducted for this (see Chapter 2), and pick from a range of choices offered by the plan administrator. The good news is that in a survey done for the American Stock Exchange in June 1996, 64 percent of 800 people between the ages of 15 and 34 were using a company-sponsored retirement plan and making regular contributions. Many of these investors don't think they can count on Social Security to be there when they retire, so they're taking matters into their own hands. Forty-two percent said they were using the company plans to invest in mutual funds, and another 42 percent said they were investing in stocks of individual companies (it's likely that many of those surveyed do both).

If the people a bit older than you are doing a good job of managing their retirement benefits, that's great news for you. You'll have pals in the workplace who can give you the benefit of their experience when you sign up for these plans. And you're coming into the working world at a time when the people handling these benefits are trying to make the investing choices clearer and easier to understand, so you may not run into some of the same kinds of mistakes other investors have. On the other hand, it won't hurt you to know about some of the pitfalls that have been common so far, so that you can avoid them:

- Not investing in the plan.

- Not investing enough in the plan (see Chapter 2).

- Investing too much of your retirement money in the stock of your own company. If you have faith in your employer, that's great, but you've already got your employment eggs—your paycheck— in that basket. It might be better to put your retirement investments in other baskets. There's a variation on this situation that's worth knowing about: Maybe you can buy your company's stock at discount, sell it for full price on the market, and use the profit you create to invest elsewhere.

- Using the retirement money for other purposes. If you have an emergency like a job loss, you might want to get at 401(k) or IRA money to stay afloat. It would be better to have an emergency fund for that, but if it happens and you have no other recourse, that's the way it is. More unfortunate still is when people borrow or take money out of their retirement plan for cars or other purchases that will decrease in value. This presents them with financial penalties and erodes their retirement nest egg. They may say they'll replace the original investment, but still, they've lost the time to let that money work and generate more earnings.

Paying Down Debt as a Way of Investing

Paying off a credit card debt that's got an 18 percent interest rate attached isn't the same thing as mutual fund investing, but lots of financial advisers point out that 18 percent is more than you can earn on lots of investments, so it's better to stop spending that money. Also, a monthly credit card expense may replace the dollars you could otherwise put into a mutual fund, allowing it to grow. And of course, earlier is always better when you're looking for a time to start investing.

Still, if you have a windfall or an income tax refund, it might not be the best idea to use all that money to pay off the debt, points out Kyra Morris, a South Carolina certified financial planner. Instead, it might be better to put some toward building up an emergency fund—that guards against future credit card debt—some toward debt, and some into investing.

Action Items

Find out about any employer-sponsored retirement plans and enroll.

Think about the different things you'd like to invest for—a house, a business of your own, or financial freedom by a certain age. Write down these goals—perhaps even illustrate them with photos. This is the start of any financial plan you'll build yourself or create with the help of a professional. When it seems that investing is complicated or money is tight, return to this dream sheet of goals. This will help you keep your eyes on the prize and stay committed.

If you find investing potentially interesting as a hobby, as many people do, look into books, software, magazines, and investment clubs.

CASE IN POINT:

Investment Profile (Hypothetical)

The Mutual Fund Education Alliance says that for either single young professionals, or two-income families with one child, this would be one way to divide the investing pie. The rationale is that the growth funds will provide money for the future. The tax-exempt money market fund would be used for savings.

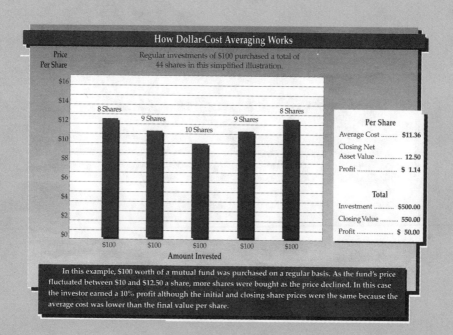

How Dollar-Cost Averaging Works

Price Per Share

Regular investments of $100 purchased a total of 44 shares in this simplified illustration.

8 Shares — 9 Shares — 10 Shares — 9 Shares — 8 Shares

Amount Invested: $100 — $100 — $100 — $100 — $100

Per Share

Average Cost	**$11.36**
Closing Net Asset Value	12.50
Profit	$ 1.14

Total

Investment	**$500.00**
Closing Value	550.00
Profit	$ 50.00

In this example, $100 worth of a mutual fund was purchased on a regular basis. As the fund's price fluctuated between $10 and $12.50 a share, more shares were bought as the price declined. In this case the investor earned a 10% profit although the initial and closing share prices were the same because the average cost was lower than the final value per share.

CASE IN POINT:

Investment Profile (Hypothetical)

(continued)

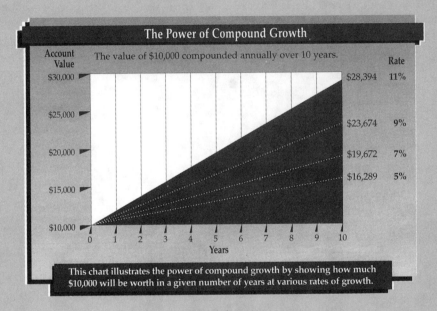

The Power of Compound Growth

Account Value — The value of $10,000 compounded annually over 10 years. — Rate

$28,394	11%
$23,674	9%
$19,672	7%
$16,289	5%

Years: 0 1 2 3 4 5 6 7 8 9 10

This chart illustrates the power of compound growth by showing how much $10,000 will be worth in a given number of years at various rates of growth.

Investing Charts provided by the Mutual Fund Education Alliance

Chapter 13

The Economy and Your Future Plans

Turn to the financial news and you will see things like the producer price index, trade deficits, purchasing managers' projections, and more. This is important data to economists, but to the layperson pursuing another career, these terms can seem remote.

Some economic news is important for you to follow, though. It can mean changes in the way you live your life, even how large a family you might want to have. The federal government figures that it costs more than half a million dollars to raise a child, which, of course, not many people have lying around. But that's what you'll spend over the years. So week to week, that demands having a source of income with good medical benefits, decent pay, enough money to provide day care if you need it, a big enough home, suitable transportation, and money for education. If, on the other hand, you are single and childless, you'll focus more on other pocketbook issues, but you'll still want to know how to make your money work the hardest for you, which careers hold the most promise, or what can you do to get the most time off if that's what you'd like. You'll never have all the information you want to make these decisions, and you'll never have it soon enough. Everything is subject to change. You'll have to make the best educated decisions you can, based on the information you can gather. The news media has been trying hard in recent years to make economics more understandable, so that should help. But don't overlook other sources of economic news either, like what your company says about the demand for its products and services, its projections for pay raises or hiring in the next year, or how it is coping with expenses. Those observations are important, although less formal, indicators of the future of your paycheck at that workplace. Another thing you'll have to keep in mind is that much of the economic news that is reported is national in scope. Employment conditions, unemployment, and pay may vary dramatically in your region of the country or field of work than the national picture shows. Some figures get reported mostly out of tradition—the daily report on the Dow Jones Industrial Average, for example, isn't even as important to active stock investors as some other measures, like The Standard & Poor's 500, which shows how part of the market for publicly owned stocks did in a given day. Even then, an isolated daily report won't solely determine how your 401(k) fares in the long run. Other kind of data can be more important to pay attention to, from developments on the job, in your city, at your bank, in Congress, or around the world.

Salary Surveys

Try to keep abreast, through the grapevine, through trade journals, and through published reports, of what people are making in your job and in other jobs that might be of interest to you. Without a good indication, you'll be at a loss to try to negotiate for a good opening pay base, or for future raises. When raises are based on percentages of your previous pay, the people who are already making more fare the best. And when you want to move to another job, the new employers frequently screen salary histories of job candidates.

Technological Advances in Your Workplace

You'll need to know if the introduction of a new computer or tool in your workplace will mean that eventually your job will disappear, or that your job category will exist, but there will be fewer people needed, or whether the industry will need people trained to use the new equipment.

Political Changes That Could Affect Your Field

Is there going to be more regulation or less? If environmental standards, for example, are decreased, and you work in that field, you might want to think about long-term job security. If you work for a tobacco company and think that antismoking sentiment will eventually erode the market for tobacco, you have to think about what that means to you personally.

Political winds aren't always running against a certain kind of job. If politicians are promising more attention to law enforcement, for example, and that's one of your interests, you'll want to know if they're specifically talking about increasing the hiring of police officers, or prosecutors, or increasing pay.

Company Mergers

Often, a new industry will create a large number of new companies. The Internet industry, for example, now has several companies participating in the field, so it looks good for job prospects now. But in a few years, the market may decide it has too many companies designing Web pages or software to surf the Web. Some will start falling away, and some will buy each other out.

If you're in this kind of a situation, your observations will have to take place on two levels. First, you want to keep abreast of the industry at large. Second, you'll want to watch what's happening at your company in particular. Sometimes a company will just announce that it's looking to be bought—other times the clues are more subtle. These clues can include lots of preoccupied senior management, top employees leaving, even visitors and unusual efforts to make the workplace neat or impressive to these visitors.

If your company buys another company, make sure you know whether there's a department like yours and anyone else doing a job like yours. You may be better off in the new structure, or you may be fired because the new company doesn't need as many people doing the same job, or because it brings in some of its own workers.

Inflation

Inflation is a standard and important statistic in reporting. Either prices are going up, down, or staying the same, but not necessarily all prices of all items are moving similarly. Sometimes you'll feel helpless when you hear an inflation report. You'll think you can't do anything about the fact that gasoline prices are increasing, for example, and that you have a 30-mile drive to work. Well, maybe you can't do anything about it. But maybe you can adjust to the circumstance, carpool, take public transportation, look for a job closer to home, or a home closer to your job. Or maybe you'll just have to stay where you are, but cut down on some other expenses so you can absorb the increase in fuel costs. That's in the short term.

In the long run, you've got to keep inflation in mind in your savings and investing activities. It's not enough for your money to grow—it has to grow enough to beat inflation. Knowing that helps you know your real rate of return. For example, if you've got money in a savings account that's earning 2 percent interest, and inflation is 3 percent, the value of your money is actually eroding with time. When you look at long-term investing, you'll want to get returns that beat inflation perhaps over the course of 20 or 30 years. In that way, inflation levels influence how aggressive you want or need to be in your investing choices.

Interest Rates

Interest rates are another statistic you may feel you have no control over, but it can be important to know what interest rates are generally in relation to the interest you're earning.

You also want to know how interest rates are moving in relation to the interest you are paying. Often credit card rates and car loans, for example, are pegged to the rates banks charge their best customers, known as the *prime rate*. Mortgage rates can be based on the interest offered on United States Treasury Bills, notes that are generally repaid to investors in three to six months. If you've got a loan with a given rate, and then interest rates start moving down, it can be worth your while to shift the debt to a new loan at a lower rate. This can be done with car and house loans, as well as with credit cards.

And if you ever lend money to someone privately, you may want to charge interest. Perhaps you'll charge the market rate at the time, or maybe you'll charge a nominal fee if it's a loan to a family member or friend, and you just want to make sure the arrangement is businesslike.

If you go into business yourself, you'll certainly want to investigate if any low-interest loans are available to you for starting up or expanding. And you may be asking bankers about revolving lines of credit that let you tap into cash when you need it for supplies, inventory, and other items.

Hometown Considerations

Are housing prices going up or down in your neighborhood? If you want to buy a house and only live in it for a couple of years, are you confident that you'll be able to get as much or more when you sell as you spent when you bought it? Now you can see why housing prices get so much attention.

If you're starting a business, or if you're an employee, you'll want to remain aware of whether your company seems to like its business environment. Can the company find the people with the skills it needs in the immediate area, for example? If transportation of materials or people into your company from out of town is important, is there adequate service for your company's needs? These are the kinds of things that influence whether companies stay or go. Local taxes can be another consideration, and they certainly get a lot of attention in the press when there's a local dispute, but these other longer-term considerations also bear watching.

Global Matters

Your job may be in Arizona, but it matters if someone in another country is doing the same work for less money. Similarly, if your company exports a lot of products, and the currency fluctuations or taxes mean that it makes it more expensive for overseas customers to buy your products, you might feel the pinch. If sales slump enough, you could even lose your job.

Not all news on the global front is going to be bad, of course. Maybe developments in another country are such that there's a widening market for the kinds of products and services your employer provides. Maybe a new job will open for you, or maybe there will be raises, or opportunities to travel.

From your investment point of view, you may find that the interest rates or industry developments in another country make for an intriguing opportunity or will spawn a new group of mutual funds you'd like to invest in.

Limited or Wide-Ranging Tax Changes

If policy makers change the way Social Security is handled, it can mean a short-term change in your take-home pay, and it could mean a different reality for your future years than what you imagine. There are, of course, other considerations to keep in mind, but in thinking about just a few of the developments that you might see in the world, you can come to grips with the fact that economics is nothing if not interrelated with the social, political, and environmental influences of the time. Your personal finances, in turn, will be affected by all those influences.

At the very least then, what you want to develop is an eye for looking at changes in the world around you and a capacity for wondering how those changes will play into economic and financial events. You won't have answers, most of the time, but you'll have the right questions. You'll get a sense of whom to ask for the best information, as opposed to an excited opinion. You'll develop a taste for the media that covers these events in the terms most meaningful to you. You will start to feel more capable in handling your financial matters and all that they entail.

Action Items

Start thinking about what financial material you've been reading and sampling since you started working on the "Action Items" following Chapter 1. Review whether you've found newspapers, magazines, broadcast, or online media you like, or whether you need to keep looking for something you can regularly follow.

Action Items

(Continued)

Start working more seriously on a financial plan. Think where you'd like to be in 5 years, in 10 years, in 30 years or more. Complete a will if you don't have one. You can use software for simple documents. If you have children, you need a will to appoint guardians for them in case you die while they're still young.

....

Make a date on your calendar at least every six months to review your financial status, how you're doing on long- and short-term goals, "Action Items," and setting any new goals.

....

Realize your economic power. Consider yourself an active consumer who can influence the development of manufacturer's products, government policy, and more.

TEN COMMANDMENTS OF PERSONAL FINANCE FOR YOUNG PEOPLE

Written by Loren Dunton, Founder and President of the National Center for Financial Education

1. Thou shalt not put out more money than taken in.
2. Thou shalt spend money thinking of your future as well as your present.
3. Thou shalt remember that compound interest is never retroactive.
4. Thou shalt NOT collect credit cards nor use them carelessly.
5. Thou shalt honor always thy debts and obligations.
6. Thou shalt develop a spending plan and spend money on savings or investments.
7. Thou shalt always search for high interest rates and a good return.
8. Thou shalt live moderately today and not worship the god of materialism.
9. Thou shalt practice dollar-cost averaging in your investing.
10. Thou shalt obtain a financial education so as to be no one's fool.

Chapter 14

Stage Two: Getting Even Smarter About Earning Money

All the skills we've discussed so far will help you with the basics of getting your first career position or managing your first big move to a new home. And lots of the information will be useful throughout your career, as negotiating skills and wise shopping practices, for instance, are constant requirements in a consumer's life. They fit in with the core fundamentals of understanding the workings of personal finance.

After a time, though, you'll want to know more than the basics of understanding what's on your paycheck stub. You'll want to know more about creating earnings power, maintaining it and improving upon it. You'll gradually acquire a greater concern for the possessions and earnings ability you have, and what it would take to replace them if some disaster struck. If you marry and start a family, as many people are expected to—take a look at the Family Planning Chart below—you'll move into a more complex scenario. If there are two income earners in the household, you'll start to compare who has the better benefits package and which health insurance plan is the most reasonable for your situation. You'll look at the cost of day care and find it makes a big difference to you whether or not your employer offers on-site day care. You'll begin to think of the importance of how geographically convenient and cost accessible any day care is.

It's impossible to generalize when these matters will become more important to you. Some people will feel this information need as soon as they get out of college, particularly if they already have a spouse or children, or are soon planning on that. Other young people may be living a single existence and just want to concentrate on their first entry level job for a couple of years or more. If you fall into that category, you may want to consult the next few chapters again in the next couple of years.

What is certain is that somewhere along the line, you will gradually acquire even more financial sophistication just from handling money and from participating in the marketplace. At the same time, events will prompt you to become more financially sophisticated—not necessarily an investment hobbyist—but someone who wants to protect their hard-earned money and make the best use of it. To return to the car analogy used in Chapter 1, driving may not inspire you to become a mechanic, but your experiences with your first car may teach you to be even more diligent with your second car—changing the oil, preventing rust, and catching mechanical problems before they turn into disasters on the side of a busy freeway. So, too, it is with jobs and the money you earn from them. You start to look for ways to protect and preserve what you've been able to accomplish.

Working to Keep Working

These days, when people can have not only several jobs, but a few different career paths over the course of a working life, it's essential to keep yourself attractive to employers. Many people think that's the only kind of employment security there is. Or to put it another way, nurturing your earnings potential is a bit like minding the fabled goose that lays the golden eggs. If you kill the goose, you can forget about that ongoing supply of valuable eggs.

Naturally, for many people, it's too soon at the start of your working career to have a detailed game plan about what employer you'll be with in several years, or to be sure about what you'll be earning. But what you can do now is realize that your career and income earnings efforts will likely accelerate over time. Sure, there may be dips if you lose a job, but generally you want to focus on an upward trend, as you can see in the following table showing earnings data from 1994. What you can do now is adopt a useful, practical mindset for advancing your goals.

How Earnings Advance with Age Until Retirement Years 1994 Data	
Median Household Income	$32,264
Income by Size of Household	
One Person	$16,222
Two People	$33,955
Income by Age of Householder	
Ages 15 to 24	$19,340
Ages 25 to 34	$33,151
Ages 35 to 44	$41,667
Ages 45 to 54	$47,261
Ages 55 to 64	$35,232
Ages 65 and older	$18,095

Source: U.S. Census Bureau Data

Thinking Like an Employer

While you're being what you consider to be a good employee, the wise thing to do is learn to look at the world the way your career field employers do and see what they value in an employee. That's not quite as simple or obvious as it sounds. Showing up on time and producing the goods is only part of the picture. That's adequate, not good. You want to know what your employer considers good enough to make you someone the workplace wants to retain, give raises to, even promote. Observe which people seem to be regarded as the most important employee assets. What skills do they have? What kinds of assignments have they taken on? Who have they worked for or with? How is the work evaluated? Are there personal skills that are especially prized?

This sounds a lot like office politics, and it is. But there's also a large measure of simply finding out what the job expectations are in a particular place. And those aren't always well articulated or communicated. You'll probably see lots of examples in your working life when a supervisor thought an employee's job emphasized one set of priorities, but the employee, perhaps being the person on the front line facing customers, would tell your differently. It's important to keep good communications open to bridge any perception gaps. Sometimes you've just got to ask your bosses and co-workers lots of questions over time about what they liked and didn't like about the way a particular project went, and how they might like to see it work differently the next time.

The skills you'll need will be tied closely to the results employers want, even though they may not always spell this out clearly in advance of your first work evaluation. Sometimes the skills employers want evolve over time, as circumstances change, customer bases shift, and projects become more complicated. It won't always be crystal clear to you at the start of each work year what will occur and what you should do to stay sharp. You'll have to adapt to conditions as they shift. For instance, 68.8 percent of the workers with bachelors degrees were using computers in 1993, according to the United States Center for Education Statistics, and we can assume the proportion is just as high today. But are they still using the same software programs? In many cases, no. A new program or a new development language may come onto the market that becomes important for your employer to use. You can make yourself valuable by adapting at least as quickly as everyone else to the new standard.

To look at a different kind of situation, say there's an increasing population in your employer's customer or client base that communications in a language other than English. Wouldn't it be in your best interest to start learning that language, too— whether it's Spanish, Chinese, or American Sign Language—if you don't already know it?

Building Your Skills Outside the Workplace

Your place of employment isn't the only venue where you can work on committees, write brochures, research new databases, devise marketing plans, evaluate an employee, or tackle other kinds of tasks that will enhance your overall attractiveness as a worker. And the job site itself isn't the only place where you can look for role models or mentors.

Lots of people have developed these skills or identified mentors by volunteering on boards or committees for community nonprofit agencies, or by taking on shorter-term assignments in various volunteer capacities. Sometimes opportunities will crop up at work or within an industry group for employment-centered endeavors or community outreach projects. But keep an eye out, too, for other opportunities in a community, religious, or other organization that might cultivate your as yet underdeveloped skills.

Thinking Like an Independent Agent

To make yourself a more prized employee in your place of work, you need to find out how your supervisors think and make decisions. But your universe doesn't stop there, of course.

To be the most nimble, employable person you can be, you also want to keep abreast of what other potential employers are seeking. Again, that's not always easy from the outside looking in. Sometimes books and magazines that rate or describe employers will give you some information, but bear in mind, that's only a thumbnail sketch. The company that appears to be casual because it allows workers to come in dressed in jeans may in fact be very rigorous about deadlines and workloads. Or you may find that a company or employer has one image that's true for much of the environment there, but that conditions are better or worse in certain departments, branch offices, or under certain supervisors. Or you may find that a distant office of a company or subsidiary operates differently than the headquarters.

From time to time, also, conditions may change the face of an employer. A downturn might freeze salary levels and new job openings for awhile, and therefore make it more difficult for people to advance for a couple of years. And a strong demand for business, while generally seen as good news, might put new responsibilities on workers' shoulders, whether or not their pay has yet increased to match the expanded role.

Generally try to keep abreast of working conditions in your field by keeping up with trade publications, news reports in the local press, and most of all, by making contacts in your field who can tell you more about the world they work in. That's one part of the equation. Then look at where you are in your own workplace, and consider what kind of shifts you could make, if you had to or wanted to. Think about whether your present situation is a good one to progress in, or whether a new climate might be more fertile grounds for you.

Then think again about your own value as an employee in the general marketplace, and whether you need to enhance what you have to offer. That's a broad way of looking at your situation, so to make the process easier, think from time to time about the answers to questions like these:

- If the company were not here tomorrow, or next month, or next year, how would I earn my living?

- If the company were purchased tomorrow, would my skills be sharp enough or so sought after that I'd stand a good chance of keeping a job in the new or merged organization?

- If my boss or mentor left tomorrow without me, would that change my future here?

- If the account/project/community I serve took their business or needs elsewhere tomorrow, would another part of my organization want me to join their staff?

If you run through these questions and come up with answers that are negative or unclear, the chances are that you're economically more vulnerable than you want to be. After all, if you can't come up with a good economic reason why your employer should keep you in pinch, or you can't imagine another employer wanting to snap you up if your employer furloughed you and other workers, you're living in ranks of the easily replaceable. Don't stay there.

Taking a Job Elsewhere

If you do move from one job to another, try to do so while preserving as many of your job related benefits as you can. If you've banked vacation days, for instance, see how many days or how much pay you have coming and factor that into planning not only your departure, but your budgeting until the first paycheck from the new job arrives. There may be a lag, depending upon how the paycheck periods run at your new employer.

Check with both benefits offices to see how to best handle your health insurance coverage, assuming you have it in both places. If there will be a gap in your coverage, you may have the option of continuing coverage from your old employer at your expense for the duration of the gap, advises Peter Wright, principal in the Boston area office of benefits consulting firm Hewitt Associates. You generally have 60 days to decide to do this, he notes, so you can try and get by without coverage, and then pay the premiums if it turned out you needed it. Still, it might be awkward to arrange treatments with patchy-looking insurance coverage, he notes. If you have some sort of pre-existing condition that requires medical treatment, like asthma, get a certificate of coverage from your old employer. Then you'll be able to present that to your new coverage providers, Wright says. That might help you get treatment for the condition under the new plan immediately or quicker than would otherwise have been available.

Got any money in flexible spending plans? See what the rules are at the employer you're departing for using up the money. You may still be able to use money in an account for dependent care after your departure, Wright says. If it's an account for medical expenses, see if you've submitted all the bills you have that could have been covered by that account.

If you've got any money in a 401(k) or other portable pension plan, Wright says, you may have a number of choices. Some companies may let you leave the money in that plan, but it may well be preferable to move it. The trick is handling the move correctly. You don't want the money to go directly to you, because you'll be taxed on it. Instead, you want to roll it directly into a 401(k) at your new employer, if they have one and allow that, or into an Individual Retirement Account. If you put the money in an IRA, Hewitt advises, put it in a "conduit IRA" that's separate from any others. That way, later, you may be able to take that sum and roll it into a 401(k) at your new company, if conditions change, or at yet another employer you might work for down the line. But if you mix the money with funds in another IRA account, it has to stay there. If you're unclear on how to arrange the precise details of these moves, talk to your human resources officer, and/or an accountant.

Action Items

Keep your attitude grounded: Remember that work is what you do to earn money and hopefully to use some of your talents, but it's not the sum of who you are.

....

Keep your resume updated.

....

Review your emergency fund to see if its adequate to cover your expenses if your unemployed; if not, make it a goal to add to the fund and keep it in liquid assets.

....

Periodically take time to reflect on what you've been accomplishing at work that will help you as well as your employer. Have you made any improvements in the way you manage your time or learned a new software program, for example? If you're not making any headway, review what short-term, concrete goals you can set for yourself.

....

Use good judgment in deciding whether to share your goals with your supervisor. Some bosses might not appreciate an employee's ambition if they think the employee is too eager to aim for a higher position. It can be wiser to confide your plans to a mentor outside the company and point out your accomplishments to your supervisor as you achieve them or when you are going through a job evaluation.

....

Learn how hiring and advancement is accomplished in your industry, for instance, whether or not recruiters are used. Stay current and keep networking.

Chapter 15

Your Maturing Financial Profile
on the Homefront

Our lives get more complicated as we
progress on life paths. You may start out single, living in a studio apartment, going to
work on public transit with your lunch packed in a knapsack. Eight years later, you
might find yourself married, leaving a house in the morning with a child to buckle into
a car seat for the drive to daycare before you head into work. You may still be carrying
your lunch in your knapsack, but you're carrying a bag for the child, too, containing
bottles, diapers, pacifiers, and assorted other baby gear that takes up an amazing
amount of space.

Or you may still be single but living in a condo or a better apartment with your gad-
gets and stuff. They include a stereo, TV, VCR, microwave, answering machine/phone
equipment, home computer, finally a good couch, and assorted other furniture, books,
clothing, and kitchenware. You might like to take a nice vacation this summer, and you
mull that over on your way to work. Still, you've been having some expensive dental
work done that you couldn't afford before, so you're not going anywhere too expensive.

That's how our money lives get more complicated: The rest of our lives acquire more texture and facets, and there are usually financial considerations attached to each turn in the road. It's important to consider, too, that in the scenarios described above, we've only looked so far at the present-day finances of these young people. We haven't yet thought about what they might be saving for retirement or if the parents have started to put away for the baby's college education yet. Don't laugh. With the price of education, your best bet is to start putting away money for children's schooling even before they're in pull-up diapers. Even if they don't go to college, or get some sort of post-high school education, a nest egg is advisable for most children. It could help them travel, set themselves up in their own home with an emergency fund eventually, or start their own studio or business. You don't know exactly what surprises the next generation may have in store, but it's a safe bet that having some money put aside will help.

Family Planning

By the year 2000, the U.S. Census Bureau predicts, 67 percent of people between the ages 25 to 34 will have been married at some point. If and when a married couple has a child, the financial picture immediately grows more complicated. Costs quickly run into the thousands for the yearly expenses that a child needs, according to government data. Those needs include adequate family housing, food, transportation, health care, clothing, child care, education, and miscellaneous expenses, such as entertainment and reading materials.

Below is a snapshot of results from a 1995 survey from the U.S. Department of Agriculture. It shows the amount of money couples with two children spent that year to support the younger of their two children. If you want to find the costs of supporting two children, just add the amounts from the appropriate age groups. For an only child, take the amount shown and multiply it by 1.24.

Age of child	Annual income less than $33,700 (Average: $21,000)	Annual income $33,700 to $56,700 (Average: $44,800)
0 to 2 years	$5,490	$7,610
3 to 5 years	$5,610	$7,810
6 to 8 years	$5,740	$7,870
9 to 11 years	$5,770	$7,860
12 to 14 years	$6,560	$8,580
15 to 17 years	$6,460	$8,710

So how do people with the fundamental money-earning and money-management skills integrate the more complex family and home situations they'll develop? Sometimes it seems like a puzzle, but other people hold some of the pieces as you try to put together the most balanced, reasonable picture.

Talking and Negotiating More About Money

Indeed, other people are holding some of the puzzle pieces. They're earning money or incurring expenses along with you, or they have some of the information you want, or exert some influence upon the homefront. So you not only have to think more about money as you advance along your earnings path, often you have to develop your capacity to discuss the subject in detail with other people. Even if you remain single and eventually seek the help of financial advisers, like budget counselors, loan officers, tax accountants, certified financial planners, or others, you're going to have to be able to identify and articulate your financial goals, your tolerance for taking risk with investments, your lifestyle and spending habits, and more. Even though people can be uptight about money, talking about all these issues is positive. Often, having to describe your goals to another person will force you to more clearly identify those goals in your own mind. And having a trusted, capable financial professional can give you a feeling of having someone on your team, someone who wants you to achieve your goals in life.

If you become part of a couple, you take on even more responsibility to talk calmly and honestly with your partner about money matters. You'll need to recognize that the other person may not have the same feelings you do about spending or saving, setting priorities, or taking risk with money. Of course, your first clue will be in actual events, and your responses, which may sound like: You mean you clip coupons? Fishing equipment costs how much? You bought this before it went on sale? Although these are surprising discoveries to lots of people, the true revelation—and the temptation to judge—comes from realizing that their partner isn't exactly like them on such issues. Such differences can be startling, but they're pretty ordinary. And their unveiling doesn't necessarily mean you now have the go-ahead to convert your partner to a better way of functioning—your way. Trying to do so may be disastrous—even adopting that attitude may be ill advised. You'll need to find a way to discuss money matters and work through both partner's thoughts and plans. This will come up all the time, whether you're thinking about whether you're choosing between two cars to purchase or looking for a good deli with reasonable prices, so you might as well get used to it.

If you have children, you'll have to decide what example you want to set for them in your money handling at the grocery store, at the toy store, at holidays and birthdays. Eventually, you'll have to decide whether and how to handle an allowance for the child, how much to advise them on making purchases, and how much freedom to allow them in making their own mistakes. This is a discussion that could include not only you and the child and the other parent, but other family members such as grandparents, aunts, and uncles. And it's likely to be an ongoing set of negotiations. It's generally better advised to think through your values and be able to articulate them calmly and firmly rather than expecting other people to know what you think or to indulge in a knee-jerk reaction if someone does something you don't agree with, like demanding the most expensive sneakers or buying your child extravagant toys without consulting you.

Even a divorce or a split up between a couple won't preclude the need for some money discussions. There's the very act of deciding who gets what, and in a legal divorce, you may have to sort out issues of taxes, property, and pensions. If there are children involved, the money discussions revolving around child support will continue indefinitely. Count on it.

Better Protecting the Household

As your earning power grows, as your lifestyle and perhaps other people become more dependent upon the fruits of your labor, you start to think more about protecting what you've already amassed. Insurance comes into your mind more often and starts to look more desirable. Previously you might have thought of insurance only as an expense, like one of the costs of maintaining a car. And that's true, it is an expense, just as the spending plan worksheet suggests. But you might also start thinking more of insurance's function, of its usefulness to you as a buffer against financial hazards greater than you'd otherwise be able to absorb.

One image that's useful in thinking about insurance is a series of concentric circles. The inside of each circle is the item of real value that you want to protect. The outer circle is the insurance that buffers against ill fortune, like a moat around a castle. At the absolute core are the most important things you want to safeguard: yours and your family's health and well-being. So the circle around that contains the health insurance you need for medical care; the disability insurance that protects your earnings power; the life insurance you would need for your family's ongoing needs if you died. The next circle might be the family home and major possessions, like the car. So the insurance circle around that would be the renter's or homeowner's insurance and the auto insurance, to protect what you've got invested in these important parts of your life. You could add one more circle, as well, your retirement savings, which you could loosely consider financial insurance to protect your spending power and well-being in your future years.

With this understanding in mind, you'll want, from time to time, to look back over the insurance afforded you from your employee benefits and the insurance you've already purchased on your own, such as auto insurance, and see if you want to supplement it somehow. But how much do you need? The Institute of Certified Financial Planners offers these guidelines in a booklet called "Taking a Fiscal Inventory: How to Put Your Financial House in Order."

Circles of Protection

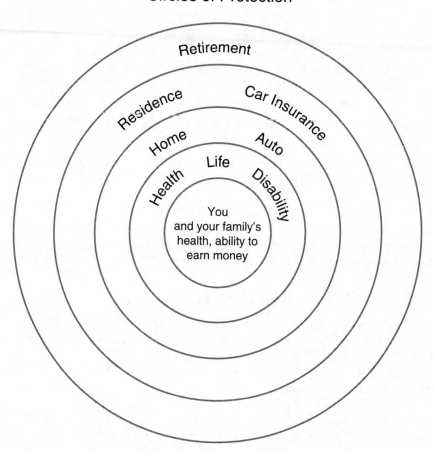

Retirement

Residence

Car Insurance

Home

Auto

Health

Life

Disability

You
and your family's
health, ability to
earn money

- Health Insurance: Everyone in the family should be covered with a major medical policy with lifetime limits of at least $1 million.

- Disability: Needed by anyone who works earning income, with enough coverage to replace 60 to 70 percent of your income should you be disabled or ill for a period of time. For many people, it's worthwhile to get coverage that specifically insures them if they can't work in their regular field—"own occupation" coverage—but might be able to work at a much lower-paying job.

- Life Insurance: Remember, it's probably not important if you're single and have no children or no one depending on you financially. If people are depening on you, figure how much income the family would have to replace to cover expenses if your income was permanently lost. A simpler rule of thumb that's often heard is to buy enough insurance to provide five to eight times your annual income.

- Homeowner's or Renter's Insurance: Go for 100 percent of the replacement costs of your items.

- Auto: Insure for $300,000 worth of bodily injury per accident, $100,000 worth of property, and $300,000 for coverage of other motorists.

Other insurance might be wise as you grow more prosperous, to cover other property and assets you accumulate, or money for nursing home care in your later years. Always comparison shop for price and coverage quality on insurance you buy on your own. An independent insurance agent who represents several different carriers can help.

Backing Up the Protection with Good Records

Once people develop a busier household, they can fall behind in their records maintenance. After all, your once-meager possessions may at one point have fit into a studio apartment, and you could practically see them all at once. It didn't take much to jot down your household inventory or put it on a computer disk. Things get more complicated when you have enough stuff for a two-bedroom place or larger. And that's only one aspect of what you need to document.

Earlier in the book, we discussed having a regular place to store your bills and paystubs. And we've mentioned some of the other documents that are important to create for yourself. Just as you think about reviewing your insurance needs and filling any gaps that may exist to protect your financial well-being, with a more complicated financial profile you'll periodically need to review your financial documents. You want to make sure they're up-to-date and stored in a safe place, with copies stored in appropriate areas. Here's a checklist:

- A worksheet of goals—where you can see it regularly.

- Warranties with receipts and dates of purchase.

- Auto records.

- Health care proxy, appointing someone to make health-care treatment decisions for you, as per your instructions, if you're too ill to communicate. Ask your doctor how these instructions are compiled in your state.

- A power of attorney document designating someone to handle any financial or legal affairs for you if necessary. This person would also need a notebook listing all your banking and financial accounts.

- A will, especially if you have children, to appoint a guardian in case you die. Even if you don't have children or a spouse, you might create a will to make sure your assets are divided according to your wishes, and not under the general guidelines your state issues when someone dies without a will. Also, make sure the details of your will make sense and are in agreement with the provisions you made for beneficiaries of life insurance policies, for instance.

- Insurance policies.

- A home inventory, with a copy stored someplace else and regularly updated.

- Records of home improvement with the costs recorded.

- Back tax returns for six years.

- Student loan records.

- A copy of your credit report.

- Investment records.

- Banking records and a spending plan blueprint.

- Any documents you might use for identification or family purposes, such as birth or death certificates or passports.

- A list of your wallet contents with phone numbers to call to report missing elements.

Many financial advisers also like the idea of creating a net worth statement while you're doing your financial housekeeping. This is like a financial scorecard that tallies what you own, such as equity in property, investments, and savings, and compares it with what you owe. That would be your debts, including, say, mortgage payments, student loans still owed, credit card balances, and so on.

This is more useful, though, when you've made more progress in your financial life. If you just got out of college with $11,000 in student debt or just got your first home mortgage for $70,000, say, it's quite likely that you owe more than you actually own. Dwelling on that or becoming frightened by it isn't really useful. As you accumulate equity in a home and amass retirement savings and stay ahead of debt, however, it can be interesting to look at your net worth from time to time to make sure you're gaining financial ground.

But even if you don't do a net worth statement and just start with assembling these other documents, you can take a step back and see how much you've accomplished. You've started earning a living and acquiring the tools to run your financial affairs so that they don't run you. Congratulations.

Action Items

Reflect periodically on your style of handling money and the values you hold around money.

....

Review your goals and enjoy your accomplishments.

....

If you have trouble discussing money with a partner, try to find out more about your different backgrounds and how they affect your views on money. Learn more about how to make two different styles work together.

Chapter 16

Dos and Don'ts and Remedies

Do make the effort to gain financial literacy.

Don't assume your finances will take care of themselves.

Remedy: Do pay attention to media coverage of personal finance issues that you can relate to.

Do make sure you're using your employee benefits as much as possible.

Don't waste benefits by overlooking them or misusing 401(k) money.

Remedy: If you're not sure about what you're entitled to, check with your company and find out the procedures for signing on for more benefits.

Do track your cash flow and shop around for the best, most convenient, and most affordable banking services package.

Don't put up with higher rates for services than you need to.

Remedy: Look into credit unions and other low-cost financial institutions.

Do make a realistic spending plan, taking into account expenses that happen only periodically, as well as savings.

Don't just let the money spend itself.

Remedy: Use a money tracking notebook for a couple of months, or a computer program to help you get a better handle on your finances.

Do make sure you're using the wisest repayment schedule for your student loans.

Don't allow yourself to fall behind on payments.

Remedy: Consider consolidation of loans if it makes sense for you.

Do keep only a couple of credit cards and pay balances promptly.

Don't fall into the trap of paying only the minimum due each month.

Remedy: Ask for help from budget counselors if credit cards are a big temptation for you.

Do shop with a list and compare prices.

Don't be seduced by slick advertising or spend money to improve a bad mood.

Remedy: Confine your shopping to specific days, use consignment shops, and think about a purchase overnight.

Do get into a regular savings and investing habit.

Don't assume this is something you can make up for in later years.

Remedy: If it's hard to save, try automatic deductions.

Do keep abreast of economic developments around you.

Don't assume that the economy doesn't affect you.

Remedy: Read the business page of a newspaper regularly.

Do everything you can to enhance your earnings power.

Don't let your skills slip or atrophy.

Remedy: Establish goals for improving your work abilities.

Do protect your family and your financial accomplishments.

Don't overlook important legal protections or insurances.

Remedy: Take stock of your financial household periodically to preserve and enjoy what you've accomplished.

INDEX

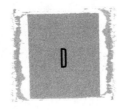

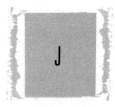

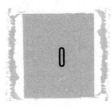

Notes